To See Clearly

Also by Suzanne Fagence Cooper

Pre-Raphaelite Art in the Victoria & Albert Museum

Effie Gray

To See Clearly
Why Ruskin Matters

SUZANNE FAGENCE COOPER

Quercus

First published in Great Britain in 2019 by Quercus.

Quercus Editions Ltd
Carmelite House
50 Victoria Embankment
London EC4Y 0DZ

An Hachette UK company

HB ISBN 978 1 78747 698 1
Ebook ISBN 978 1 78747 699 8

10 9 8 7 6 5 4 3 2

Picture credits: pages 11, 23, 43, 67, 89, 139, 191 © and courtesy of the
Ashmolean Museum, University of Oxford. Pages 115, 163 © and courtesy
of the Ruskin Library and Research Centre, Lancaster University.

Typeset by CC Book Production
Printed and bound in Great Britain by Clays Ltd, Elcograf S.p.A.

For my beloved girls, Rosalind and Beatrice

Contents

Preface:

Venetian Glass

John Ruskin feels the smooth glass beads in his hand, turning them over with his fingertips. Indigo blue, scarlet, buttercup yellow and grass green – miniature rainbows. He looks at them intently, and lifts them up to the light. Then he begins to write.

He describes, with barely suppressed rage, how these beads are made: how the rods of glowing glass 'are chopped up into fragments . . . by the human hand', and how these hands vibrate 'with a perpetual and exquisitely timed palsy, and the beads dropping beneath their vibration like hail'. He has seen the process with his own eyes, when he visited the workshops of Murano, and he cannot unsee the dreadful conditions in which these tiny baubles were made. He declares that 'every young lady, therefore, who buys glass beads is engaged in the slave-trade'.[1] Take responsibility, he insists. Don't look away.

Clearly, urgently, Ruskin speaks to us. He shows that we are all connected by our choices – what we wear and eat and read, how we travel, how we spend our money, how we teach our children.

Ruskin understands how people are affected by places, how the landscape shapes us, and how we change our environment. He gave us an early warning about climate change – having watched the skies, and painted the dawn since he was a boy, he woke up to the 'Storm-Cloud' of pollution lowering overhead. Look at the world, he says, look at this leaf, this bird's wing, this mountain. He encourages us to share his love of the natural world, his delight in paintings and buildings and beautiful books. He opens our eyes, showing us new ways of seeing. In Ruskin we find a freshness, a vulnerability, and then a descent into silence.

My own encounter with Ruskin began as a teenager. I was swallowed up by *The Stones of Venice*, as some of my friends became absorbed by Middle Earth. Here was a new immersive world, where every detail of a building or a view could tell a story about people who were here before me. For Ruskin, beauty was not neat; it could be savage, grotesque, changeful, on the point of bursting into full bloom, but never florid or decadent. He offered a new way of experiencing and interacting.

As William Morris, the poet/maker said, Ruskin seemed 'to point out a new road on which the world should travel'. He made it possible for me to say, as Morris said, that I wanted to 'devote my life to art'. To be an art historian, searching for beauty and pointing it out to others, no longer seemed impossible. It seemed essential, a vocation, a way of connecting the present to the past. Standing outside the cathedral in Pisa last year, asking my students to look closely at the surface of the curved apse, and the intricate carvings tucked high up under the roofline, I shared with them Ruskin's watercolour of the same scene, made 160 years before. With his help, they saw that the stones were not plain white, but full of mother-of-pearl complexities – pale pinks and soft golds, with silvery-blue veins. This was all new. For some, it was life-changing. As Ruskin put it, 'To see clearly is poetry, prophecy, and religion, – all in one.'[2]

He doesn't make it easy for us. His titles are off-putting. What should we expect to find in books called *Fors Clavigera*, or *Unto this Last*? How can the twenty-first-century reader know that *Fors* was written like a blog, that it is a series of essays or 'think pieces' about the issues that bothered Ruskin and his world, a newsletter updated every few weeks that shows us the workings of Ruskin's mind? He was wonderfully connected, weaving together stories across boundaries of discipline, language, century. In the blink of an eye, Ruskin leads us from the very small – the contemplation of the intense blue petals of a gentian – to the colossal: an alp, a cathedral, the flight of an eagle across a whole continent.

In our age of immediacy, Ruskin encourages us to linger. We wonder with him at the beauty before our eyes. Often accused of being scared of sensuality, a critic of the 'fleshly' art of the Renaissance, he offers us an alternative sensuality of vision. He was, in every sense, a visionary. As a young man he wrote with pleasure, for example, of a landscape, where 'every line is voluptuous, floating, and wavy in its form; deep, rich, and exquisitely soft in its colour; drowsy in its effect; like slow wild music; letting the eye repose on it, as on a wreath of cloud'.[3]

Still, he needed action, not just words. He scrambled up scaffolding to argue with the French demolition team who were taking sledgehammers to sculptures on an ancient church. He saw the potential in new technologies, as an early adopter of photography to record the crumbling carvings, the exact shapes and shadows on a beloved building. He was outspoken in anti-vivisection campaigns, and gave up his post as Slade Professor of Fine Art in protest when he heard that the new science labs at Oxford would be used for animal testing. He climbed mountains and dug foundations.

Ruskin also shared with us the fragility of his own mental health. With terrible clarity he knew that he was going under. His description of the process of losing his mind is chilling. Watching over his shoulder as he writes his diary, we see the connections begin to unravel – all the threads of thought, which he had once been able to knit together for his reader, now tangled and impossible to follow. His mania, his loss of faith – at some level these were the flip side of his desire to explain the workings of the world, the interconnectedness of the spirit and the senses. Churchill had his 'Black Dog' of depression. Ruskin describes a black cat leaping out, a physical struggle, and finding himself naked and alone in the early morning. He was vulnerable and at times deeply troubled.

Ruskin was not infallible. His uncomfortable attitudes to women and sex have come to define him to many. We must acknowledge his impotency, address his fixation on young girls. He was an inspired and inspiring writer, but a dreadful husband. His biography, at one level, is a history of failed and flawed personal relationships. He struggled against the repressive love of his parents, distanced himself from his wife, lost his beloved Rose. He misjudged many contemporary artists, including James Whistler, and alienated old friends.

But his prickliness made him ask the big questions: about relationships between workers and management; about education and training and freedom of expression. What is truth, what is faith? What is money, what is power? How should we look after our old people? Does the free market work? His words overturned political certainties. When the pioneers of the British Labour movement were asked to name the most influential books that had brought them into politics, Ruskin was their first choice. Not Dickens, or even the Bible, but Ruskin.

His essays in *Unto this Last* had a similar impact – 'an instantaneous and practical transformation' – on the life of the young Gandhi. It was, he said 'The Magic Spell of a Book'. Ruskin convinced Gandhi that 'there is no wealth but life'.[4]

7

Gandhi kept thinking about Ruskin throughout his campaigns. In 1932, he wrote from Central Prison, Poona, to a young woman in Britain:

Dear Sister, Whilst I was in England last Autumn some friends sent me Ruskin's *Guild of St George*. The leisure I have in this prison enabled me to read the book. Having been much influenced myself by Ruskin's *Unto this Last*, I read your account of the Guild with deep interest. I write this moment to ask if you could kindly send me a collection of Ruskin's writings in *Fors Clavigera*? Yours sincerely, M.K. Gandhi

Edith Scott could not afford to post the eight volumes to India – as Gandhi put it, 'I see you are fortunate enough to have no superfluous cash'. But she managed to arrange for the books to be sent by another, wealthier, follower of Ruskin. Reading Ruskin – in South Africa, in London, in India – was a catalyst for extraordinary change.[5]

So what can we learn from him, 200 years after his birth? We can start, perhaps, by adopting his motto: 'To-Day'. We can begin to understand:

* the ways that 'hand, head and heart' can work together
* how drawing makes us notice the overlooked

* what stories the buildings around us can tell us about the people who made them, and live in them now
* how we can travel with more care through the landscape, walking and thinking, observing the clouds, or the earth beneath our feet
* our struggles with love, and with the loss of the people and things we love
* different responses to our own mental fragility, and the anxieties of others
* possibilities for working more effectively, and more fairly
* above all, how we can keep learning, whether we are young or old, in small ways and in great, tumultuous revelations.

With our eyes opened by Ruskin's fierce words, we can look about us and face up to the responsibilities of our interconnected world.

Introduction:

How did Ruskin learn to look?

Part of the Base of a Pilaster in Santa Maria dei Miracoli, Venice

Ruskin and his parents

We know a huge amount about how Ruskin's mind works, because he wrote constantly. His collected writings fill thirty-nine fat volumes, edited after his death in 1900 by the ever-faithful pair, E. T. Cook and Alexander Wedderburn.[6]

John Ruskin was brought up in London, though his parents met and married in Perthshire. Margaret Cox and John James Ruskin were cousins, and she had come to Scotland to act as companion to her aunt. Margaret was the daughter of a pub landlord in Croydon, and her sense of social inferiority cast a long shadow. John James inherited a sherry importing business after his own father committed suicide in 1817. This meant that Ruskin's upbringing was tinged with his parents' memories of madness and fear of bankruptcy, with the added class anxiety of being 'in trade'.

John Ruskin was a late and only child, born in 1819 when his mother was thirty-seven. He was mostly taught at home, with tutors for drawing, Greek and Latin. But he admitted that as a young man, he 'was allowed without remonstrance to go on measuring the blue of the sky, and watching the flight of the clouds, till I had forgotten most of the Latin I ever knew, and all the Greek'.[7] His parents enjoyed travelling and had the money to hire the most comfortable carriages, so some of Ruskin's earliest memories were of looking over hedges from his own little high seat at the landscapes of the Lakes or Wales. His affection for the old ways wells up in his description of one of these journeys in a marvellous carriage, with 'store-cellars under the seats, secret drawers under front windows, invisible pockets under padded lining, safe from dust ... the fitting of cushions where they would not slip, the rounding of corners for more delicate repose; the prudent attachments and springs of blinds'. The family would set out in late spring, after his father's birthday, 'in the midst of hawthorn, laburnum, and lilac blossom'.[8]

One remarkable year, 1833, he and his father treated themselves to a collection of prints of *Flanders and Germany* by Prout. That evening, as father and son shared their new treasure, Margaret suggested, 'Why should not we go and see some of them in reality? My father hesitated a little, then with glittering eyes said – why not?'[9] And so, after a fortnight of bustle, they were at Calais, and setting off across Europe. They outpaced Prout. Flanders and Germany were not enough. They wanted to see Mont Blanc and the Black Forest, Lucerne, Como and Milan. They reached Genoa in the middle of June. There Margaret Ruskin found that the heat was too much for her, and they turned for home. But the Alps had worked their magic. For John the sight of the mountains was a revelation: 'They were clear as crystal, sharp on the pure horizon sky, and already tinged with rose by the sinking sun. Infinitely beyond all that we had ever thought or dreamed'. It was a Sunday. Many years later, he wrote, 'To that terrace, and the shore of Lake Geneva, my heart and faith return to this day.' He believed, on that evening, his 'destiny [was] fixed in all of it that was to be sacred and useful'.[10]

What was this sacred and useful work? He had considered becoming 'an amiable clergyman'. He was bred, he said, for the Church. And his father could never quite accept that he had turned to writing instead. 'With tears in his eyes', he would explain that John could 'have been a Bishop'. Still, his lectures were often more pithy and devotional than the sermons he had heard as a child, and his essays were laced with Biblical allusions. John had grown up with God (and his mother) watching over him, and he wrestled with her Evangelical Christian teachings throughout his life. He was 'withdrawn from the sherry trade, as an unclean thing', to be educated as a gentleman-commoner at Christ Church, Oxford. His mother came with him. She took rooms in the High Street, and during term time he visited her every evening for tea, jogging back to college when the great bell was sounded because the gates were being shut for the night.

At the end of his life, when both his parents were dead, Ruskin wrote his memoirs, published as *Praeterita*. That is how we know so much about his childhood – or at least, one version of the story, for his retelling of his early life was sometimes accurate, sometimes overlaid by regrets or wishful thinking. Some things were best forgotten.

Ruskin and Turner

So why did Ruskin become an art critic, choosing to 'tell the public about Turner and Raphael', rather than training to be a priest?[11] He found that art was about God. And history, and growing things, and imagined marvels, and hard facts about truth and dishonesty, and the way rivers flowed, and clouds were tinted at dawn, and mountain peaks sang in the wind. Paintings and buildings were only the starting point. To explain them, to look into them and through them was to begin to understand the whole culture that created them, from a single worker to an economic system. And then there were the materials the art was made from, and the landscapes or characters they represented. And who owned them, and all the poetry and myths they sprang from. Layer upon layer of ideas and images to be sifted, and to learn from. This was the wonder of art history. It still is.

Ruskin could reach a far wider audience through his books on *Modern Painters* or *The Stones of Venice* than he could as a vicar (or even a bishop) on a Sunday morning. He never wavered from his belief that 'All great Art is Praise'[12]; this was the bedrock of his teaching. Perhaps it has also been his undoing in a post-Christian era, because he does sometimes sound too much like a preacher scolding us from the pulpit. For him, praise meant looking outwards and upwards to something more magnificent than our own little lives. It meant, as he said in *The Crown of Wild Olive*, questioning whether you believe that this world, here and now, is all there is. Or whether there is more, beyond.

His first serious piece of art criticism set the tone for his life's work. He was outraged by negative reviews of J.M.W. Turner's paintings in the 1836 Royal Academy exhibition, and decided to write a riposte. He had hoped to impress Turner by the fierce enthusiasm of his essay, but the artist was unmoved, and the piece was not published. This desire to demonstrate Turner's pre-eminence, and Ruskin's complex interaction with his readers, was a constant thread in his career. Ruskin never wrote to please. He wrote to probe and question, to stir up and to reimagine.

He devoted much of his attention from 1843 (Volume 1) to 1860 (Volume 5) to a study of *Modern Painters*. This was begun, again, as a response to Turner's recent work, but it developed into a provocative survey of art (ancient and modern), mountains, clouds, and truth to nature. Influenced by his own studies in geology and botany, as well as a belief in natural theology, Ruskin argued that 'There is a moral as well as material truth, – a truth of impression as well as of

17

form, – of thought as well as of matter'.[13] And Turner was the artist who best expressed these truths. *Modern Painters* caused a sensation. His luminous writing was, for some, revelatory. Charlotte Brontë said, 'I feel now as if I had been walking blindfold – this book seems to give me eyes.'[14] Ruskin became something of a celebrity in London intellectual circles, and began to lecture as well as write.

Ruskin and Effie Gray

In May 1848, after a brief courtship, mostly conducted by letter, Ruskin married nineteen-year-old Effie Gray. He was thirty, and had known her since she was a schoolgirl. Effie Gray turned heads. Even as a teenager, she was 'extremely admired in appearance and manners', with thick coppery plaits. Tall, confident, and the eldest of thirteen children, she was used to holding court at dinner and running the household when her mother was in confinement. Full of energy, she loved to dance and chat and travel. Effie particularly enjoyed staying with the Ruskins as they took her into London, to the theatre, and to meet artists and poets. She had stopped with them several times on her way to school in Stratford-upon-Avon. John had enjoyed her visits, and, as was his way with girls he liked, he wrote for her. His only fairy tale, *The King of the Golden River*, was a gift for the bright twelve-year-old. But the next time she visited, Ruskin already thought she was 'very graceful but had lost something of her good looks.' Effie, for her part, treated Ruskin and his parents like extended family.

The Grays and the Ruskins had been friends for many years; Effie grew up at Bowerswell, the house near Perth that had previously been owned by John James Ruskin's family. Memories of the sudden, traumatic deaths of John James's parents meant that Ruskin's mother and father did not travel to Scotland for the wedding. (Effie had been born in the same bedroom in which Ruskin's grandfather had slit his throat with a razor.)

Their engagement was short. The couple did not see each other between Ruskin's first avowal of love in the autumn and the week of their wedding the following spring. The honeymoon was marred by money worries, and both bride and groom were unwell. Their marriage was not consummated that summer. Ruskin agreed that they should try again after Effie's twenty-fifth birthday, but by then, the misunderstandings and unhappiness could not be overcome. Effie found it difficult to conform to the expectations of Ruskin's parents. They called her extravagant, and she called them interfering. Ruskin wrote later to his lawyer: 'I married her, thinking her young and affectionate that I might influence her as I chose, and make of her just such a wife as I wanted. It appeared that she married me thinking she could make of me just the husband she wanted.'[15]

In Venice, they came to a compromise. On both their visits, they enjoyed their time together and separately; Ruskin recalled his pleasure at watching Effie stand up to row a gondola, and he encouraged her to go out to parties or the theatre, often chaperoned by his new friend, a handsome Austrian officer called Charles Paulizza. Ruskin liked it when other men admired his wife. He laughed when they brought her bouquets, or tried to ingratiate their way into her opera box. As he pointed out in a letter to his father, she could 'do as she likes, so long as she does not interfere with me'. And Effie tried to explain to her mother, 'I am so peculiarly situated as a married woman, most men thinking that I live quite alone.' According to Ruskin she was 'very good and prudent'. She needed to be, as she could not risk 'the only fortune I have, viz – a good name'.[16] Increasingly she worried that her husband was trying to get her into what she called 'a scrape', some indiscretion or affair.

Effie left him in 1854, and obtained an annulment of the marriage; Ruskin did not contest the case. As a result, he was declared incurably impotent. After a decent interval, she was free to marry the young Pre-Raphaelite artist, John Everett Millais. Ruskin tried to sidestep the rumours concerning the breakdown of his marriage by travelling to the Alps with his parents, as if nothing serious had happened. In fact, his reputation was permanently scarred by the gossip associated with his sexual conduct. To this day, the only thing that many people know about Ruskin is that he never had sex with his wife. There may be some mutterings about pubic hair, based on his comment that 'though her face was beautiful, her person was not formed to excite passion'.[17]

20

Effie did have one positive effect on him, though. She twice persuaded Ruskin to move to Venice, partly to avoid his overbearing parents, but largely so that he could complete his research into Venetian Gothic architecture and society. On the back of these visits, he wrote *The Stones of Venice* and reinforced his position as a cultural commentator as well as an art critic. This work helped to lay the foundations for the Arts and Crafts Movement and established Ruskin as an engaging and controversial voice for his own generation, and many younger followers.

Ruskin and Brantwood

In later life, Ruskin moved from London to the Lakes. He watched the skies from Brantwood, his house on Coniston Water. He bought it just before his mother died in 1871. At times, his depression at the loss of his parents and his beloved Rose La Touche, the young Irish woman he had hoped to marry, developed into mania. He suffered from violent episodes, with paranoid hallucinations, and often could not work. He was looked after by his cousin, Joan Agnew and her husband Arthur Severn.

During this disjointed time he wrote his memoirs, *Praeterita*. The work was never completed. It is a poignant, partial account of his upbringing, often contradictory, sometimes extravagantly self-pitying. He never mentions Effie. But he lingers over lost loves, long walks in the mountains, and the beauty of 'leaves, and pebbles'.[18] His ability to share his delight in the small glories of the garden, as well as the great wonders of glaciers or Gothic cathedrals, makes his autobiography a joy to read. He transforms the memories of his boyhood into vivid set pieces. They may not always be entirely accurate, but that does not diminish their power. We remember his first sight of the Alps. Or his drawing of an aspen tree on a hot afternoon. Or the little boy sitting by the stream's edge, watching the water flow. Ruskin understands the lasting value of a well-told tale. He gives us a glimpse of how he came to see so clearly, to question so intensely. These moments are polished and offered to us, as treasured possessions, as part of his personal mythology. And, as he reminds us: 'Never confuse a Myth with a lie.'[19]

Chapter 1

Seeing

Quick Study of Leaf Contour: Bramble

'Free-heartedness, and graciousness, and undisturbed trust, and requited love, and the sight of the peace of others, and the ministry to their pain; – these and the blue sky above you, and the sweet waters and flowers of the earth beneath; and mysteries and presences, innumerable, of living things – these may yet be your riches'.[20]

Ruskin's care for his reader overspills the page as he calls down blessings like an ancient prophet or seer. He conjures up delights, sensual and intellectual, full of colour and movement. He encourages us to believe, with him, in a brighter world.

The view from south London

From his study window, John Ruskin looked across the suburbs of south London as he fashioned his phrases. Throughout his life, he was in the habit of watching the sun rise and set.

He observed the clouds and the direction of the wind. The outer world was just as important to him as the inner workings of his mind. And so, when he pronounced a glorious benediction on his readers, he imagined the wonders, seen and unseen, that he desired for them, as well as for himself.

In Camberwell, and in Bradford, and in Woolwich, he had harangued the audiences at his lectures. He questioned their respectable, conventional ways of 'getting on' and made them feel uncomfortable. 'What do you believe?' he demanded. Why, then, do you live like this – wastefully, selfishly, without looking about you? Now, in 1866, as he wrote up his lectures in *The Crown of Wild Olive*, he tried to explain his urgency and his rudeness. What we do matters, he tried to say. We need to look at the world more clearly. We should ask whether we help or hurt the people around us, those we rely on, those we barely notice. Above all, we should be glad in the loveliness before our eyes.

Ruskin was often told that his way of thinking 'is very beautiful but it is not practical'.[21] His critics called him naïve, as he shifted his arguments towards politics or economics. When he was invited to speak in Bradford, he understood that his audience wanted his advice on how to build their new Exchange.

> You know there are a great many odd styles of architecture . . . you don't want to do anything ridiculous; you hear of me, among others, as a respectable architectural

man-milliner; and you send for me, that I may tell you the leading fashion; and what is, in our shops, for the moment, the newest and sweetest thing in pinnacles.

He refused. Instead he turned their preconceptions upside down. The good people of Bradford assumed that 'taste is one thing, morality is another'. Ruskin insisted taste 'is the ONLY morality ... Tell me what you like, and I'll tell you what you are'. He urged them to look for loveliness, a 'simple love of that which deserves love'. He tried to explain that this 'is not an indifferent nor optional thing whether we love this or that; but it is just the vital function of all our being'.[22] It didn't really matter whether they chose a pointed arch or a round one for their Exchange. What mattered was why they were setting up the building in the first place – out of pride or envy, or as a temple for the 'Goddess of Getting-on'. So what was supposed to be a lecture on the relative merits of Gothic and Classical architecture became a fierce denunciation of the *laissez-faire* economics of merchants and mill owners, who looked after themselves but whose workers were left out in the cold.

He knew that his outspoken views made him unpopular. Even his father asked him to temper his blunt opinions and stick to talking about Turner or the Pre-Raphaelites. But he could not turn a blind eye. He knew he did not have to work for a living – his parents paid his way at every stage – but this meant that he had the time and training to give a voice to the voiceless, to see the details that other people missed, to pry and poke, and to open up the possibility of a richer life for some. This was not an easy option. He would have preferred to remain unremarked. He outlined this touchingly in his autobiography, and it explains a great deal about his gauche behaviour. As his father said, he was better on paper than in the flesh.

My entire delight was in observing without being myself noticed, – if I could have been invisible, all the better. I was absolutely interested in men and their ways, as I was interested in marmots and chamois, in tomtits and trout. If only they would stay still and let me look at them, and not get into their holes and up their heights! The living inhabitation of the world – the grazing and nesting in it, – the spiritual power of the air, the rocks, the waters, to be in the midst of it, and rejoice and wonder at it, and help it if I could, – happier if it needed no help of mine, – this was the essential love of Nature in me, this the root of all that I have usefully become, and the light of all that I have rightly learned.[23]

Of course, we cannot take his claims to objectivity at face value. Often we are the ones asking the awkward questions about his points of view. Yes, he wrote as a privileged white man. For many years he hardly ever questioned this, except

28

occasionally to discuss the education of privileged young white women. In his forties he turned his attention to the hand-makers and factory workers, speaking out against the desperate conditions created by industrial capitalism. He became a champion of clean air, education for all and fair wages. However, despite his enthusiasm for 'lifelong learning', older women are largely invisible in his writings. This is one element of the status quo that he failed to question. He was an outspoken opponent of empire at times, yet there is a deeply ingrained racism in much of his writing about colonialism. We could say that, in these prejudices, he was no worse than Dickens or Gladstone or Tennyson, or most of his generation. But that is not enough. Our job now is to respond to him by pushing back his boundaries and seeing further than he did.

Learning to look

From his apartment in Venice, in the winter of 1850, he had tried to encourage his readers: 'You were made for enjoyment,' he wrote, 'and the world was filled with things which you will enjoy, unless you are too proud to be pleased by them, or too grasping to care for what you cannot turn to other account than mere delight.' He urged his audience to 'Remember that the most beautiful things in the world are the most useless; peacocks and lilies for instance'. He went on: 'At least I suppose this quill I hold in my hand writes better than a peacock's would, and the peasants of Vevay, whose fields in spring time are white with lilies ... told me the hay was none the better for them'.[24]

Peacocks and lilies would later become associated with luxurious love of beauty for its own sake. But for Ruskin, looking at a lovely thing was always more than self-indulgence. He taught us that it is worthwhile, and uplifting, and right to look for the well formed, the kindly weathered, the small and unexpected visual treats that are right here. There is beauty and interest in a brick wall or a weed, maybe not as much as in the mosaics and domes of St Mark's in Venice, but certainly something to catch our eyes.

Ruskin grew up having little to look at. He remembered tracing the colours of the carpet and the knots in the wooden floor, because he was expected to 'find [his] own amusement' and had few toys – a cart, a ball and, when he was five or six, a set of wooden building blocks.[25] He explained that he learnt an early lesson of 'narrowing myself to happiness within the four brick walls' of his mother's garden.[26] Within this small space, he found enough to admire in 'a strong old mulberry tree, a tall white-heart cherry tree, a black Kentish one, and an almost unbroken hedge, all round, of alternate gooseberry and currant bush'. The colours of the fruit still tingle in his memory: 'fresh green, soft amber, and rough-bristled crimson ... clustered pearl and pendant ruby'. And then comes the most telling detail. He imagines it as the Garden of Eden, except that 'in this one, all the fruit was forbidden; and there were no companionable beasts'.[27]

We can never forget that his mother had schooled him thoroughly, so that he knew long passages of the Bible by heart. He wrote and thought and saw inevitably through the prism of the Old and New Testaments, and the Book of Common Prayer. In the rise and fall of his phrases we find constant echoes of the King James translation. But it was not just the Bible that shaped his view of the world. He was well versed in Byron and Dante, Homer, Virgil and Scott. Their many voices overlap Ruskin's own experience, welling up through his sentences so often that he barely acknowledges their presence. They are part of his make-up, and underpin his complex patterns of thought.

He is the master of interdisciplinarity, a man whose mind could dart about, from now to then, from here to there, from text to image to building to rock formation, with marvellous felicity. And he draws us in his wake, opening up fresh visions and calling us to action with his constant questions and explanations. He never expects us to know as much as he does. But he never talks down to us either. As long as his mind holds firm, he is an excellent guide, saying time and again, 'Have you seen this? Have you thought about this? Because I have, and I think you should too. I've found something important, and no one else seems to have noticed.'

Ruskin recognised that the world was changing fast. He knew that he could not take for granted the certainties that had kept his parents in their old-fashioned, unhurried lifestyle. He knew that he was privileged, and that he was peculiar. Looking back, he said that he was happiest when his life was 'most regular and most solitary'. But he made his 'not fitting in' work in his favour. He could cross boundaries and voice his opinions, at first on art, but then increasingly he spoke out about the Alps, pollution, economics, war, railways, women's education, the good and ill he saw in the world. He can still teach us about the interconnectedness of people and things and places, if only we know how to look. This is the essence of Ruskin: his ability to make connections, and to show us why they matter.

Sometimes it seems that Ruskin privileges sight to the exclusion of other sensory possibilities. When he was asked if he would contribute to a charity for the blind, he said no. His business, he believed, was with people who were unwilling to engage – 'who have eyes and see not' – rather than those who were living with a physical disability.[28] However, according to the scholar Stuart Eagles, who is sight impaired, Ruskin's work often suggests that insight and keen vision are not necessarily bound up with physical looking. His writings and lectures enable access to 'a visual world that is beautiful, even if for some of us it exists largely in the imagination, rather than sensed experience or even memory'. And Ruskin's words deserve to be read aloud. Not just the lectures, but the prose pictures offer a way to appreciate 'lyrical beauty . . . far beyond mere physical sight'.[29] When Ruskin describes Turner or Veronese, 'he repaints the canvases, even for those with excellent sight'. He seems to see more clearly than the rest of us.

Watching the water flow

Looking can be the first step to falling in love. Or it can make us ask how something is made. Or who made it. Or why. Seeing the ground beneath our feet or the sky above helps us to feel part of an intricate network of living things – what Ruskin would call 'Creation'. And it was not just the plants and animals that drew his attention. For him, the flow of water through a landscape, the channels cut by a stream and even the rocks of the stream bed were filled with possibilities for storytelling. His first love was geology, and he was always searching for the deep history of river valleys, the movements of glaciers or the upswelling of mountains.

We have already seen that this desire to look closely at the workings of nature began early, as a toddler in his enclosed garden. His Scottish aunt also 'had a garden full of gooseberry-bushes', but hers sloped 'down to the Tay, with a door opening to the water, which ran past it clear-brown over the pebbles three or four feet deep; an infinite thing for a child to look down into'.[30] The constant swift motion, the tumbling stones, above all the sense of freedom from the constraint of his south London upbringing, combined to make this long-looking a greater delight. And he takes us with him, so that we can almost taste the sharpness of the gooseberries and feel the lap of the water at our fingertips.

Ruskin shows us what is most important about this scene.

He brings into focus the small boy, squatting on the steps, alive to the small enchantments of a quiet scene. He saw it at the time. He could recreate it in his mind's eye nearly fifty years later. And he can bring it back for us, with all its immediacy and joy.

Throughout his life, Ruskin loved the movement of water. As an old man, he built cascades behind his house at Brantwood, and as a young man, he could happily spend 'four or five hours every day in simply staring and wondering at the sea, – an occupation which never failed me till I was forty.' His mother would not allow him 'to row, far less to sail, nor to walk near the harbour alone'.[31] But he could look. And so he began to understand how water changed everything it touched, from the green edges of a riverbank to the rigging of a boat. He noticed things that other people missed. This made him an extraordinarily perceptive art critic.

When he was a teenager, Ruskin became fascinated with the prints and paintings of J.M.W. Turner. One of the reasons he admired Turner was because of the artist's 'Truth to Nature'. But even Turner failed to paint water properly. As Ruskin put it, 'I used once to think Homer's phrase "wet water" somewhat tautological; but I see that he was right.'[32] Turner's water, in many of his paintings, was not wet enough. This bothered Ruskin so much that, to complete his book on Turner and other *Modern Painters*, he checked with his friend, Oswald Brierly, a naval artist. Brierly agreed that nobody looked really wet in Turner's *Shipwreck*, and that the canvas of the upper parts of the sails in his picture of *Calais Pier* should be 'several shades lighter, and greyer or cooler' than the lower, wetter portion. He explained that 'in any ordinary breezy weather, when you see boats knocking about at Spithead, and if the sun is shining through the sails . . . the transparent wet parts give a very beautiful effect'.[33] It was this attention to detail that Ruskin looked for in his ideal artist, a sense of being out in the full breeze and splashed by the waves.

Even when Turner was painting myths and legends, Ruskin still expected him to create a backdrop that was believable. Or at least, not plain wrong. This was a particular problem when the scene contained a river. In Turner's *Garden of the Hesperides*, Ruskin recognised that the main event would be a work of the imagination – the goddess Discord, choosing an apple that would eventually be given to Helen, as the most beautiful woman in the world, and so cause the Trojan War. But first he chided Turner for painting the golden apples as 'very unripe and pale pippins', which he could not expect 'goddesses would be likely to quarrel for'. Then he was concerned that the mountainous background was merely a 'memory of the Alps': 'It is not *possible*,' he wrote, 'that hill masses on this scale, should be divided into these simple, steep, and stone-like forms. Great mountains, however bold, are always full of endless fracture and detail.' It was the water that bothered him most, though.

Looking into the depths of the painting, Ruskin felt

cheated. 'In nature,' he knew, 'that torrent would have worn for itself a profound bed, full of roundings and wrinkled lateral gulphs. Here, it merely dashes among the squared stones as if it had just been turned on by a New River company.' Turner had made no attempt to show the passing of geological time, which would have softened and eroded the river valley. Turner had visited the Alps, Wales and the uplands of northern England – so why did he not see the problem, as Ruskin did? Cutting corners, or misremembering, or not caring, were hard for Ruskin to forgive or to understand. He ends this passage of criticism in *Modern Painters* by turning back, in his own mind, to a Swiss meadow that he had seen and sketched. The mosses and *myrtilles* were there, violet and silver and green against the grey rocks. And the loveliest flower: 'the gentian's peace of pale, ineffable azure, as if strange stars had been made for earth out of the blue light of heaven'.[34] So the writing came full circle, as Ruskin recalled his beloved starry flowers, and the Hesperides themselves, daughters of the Evening Star. He knew there was a better way to paint this scene, better even than Turner: not brown and barren, but rich in colour and association, with a beautiful river gorge, blessed with flowers and fruit, running through it. This would be the perfect setting for the star girls' garden. Even if they were being watched by a scaly serpent, who guarded their golden apples.

Why should it bother us, a century and a half later, how an artist and his critic might reimagine a myth from a long-dead civilisation? Largely because Ruskin wants us to learn to keep our eyes open. He teaches us to notice the details that explain how the world works, and how it might work differently. To find where the gaps are, and to look for answers. He is never content to accept someone else's version of events. Ruskin knew that even Turner, whom he revered, could not always see the wetness of water, or the shaping of a stream bed. Turner sometimes was too conventional to look for himself – he just repeated the bad habits of earlier artists, smoothing out, idealising. This was not enough.

'Patience in looking, and precision in feeling ... formed my analytic power,'[35] Ruskin wrote in his autobiography. He analysed, he understood, he taught. Teasing out reality and truth from a mass of vague, half-formed or faked material is a skill that we all need, now more than ever. Like Ruskin, we should know what lies beneath the surface, how the traces of the past remain within the present. In simple terms, can we spot a filtered photo, or a hidden motive? Are we being fed advertising or information? Do we trust our sources? If we can't see something immediately, it doesn't mean it's not there.

There is an extraordinarily vivid example of this, which arises from Ruskin's concern about water. He writes about a walk through the uplands of the Jura, where he found an unexpected, silent landscape: 'no whisper, nor murmur, nor patter, nor song, of streamlet'. He keeps walking, over 'absolutely crisp turf and sun-bright rock, without so much water anywhere as a cress could grow in, or a tadpole wag his tail in'. He watches a rain cloud pass overhead, yet within an hour, the rocks are dry again. He looks and he thinks. He needs to know, and to tell us. This quiet plateau, he finds, is riddled with 'unseen fissures and filmy crannies'. Into these the waters vanish. And far away, 'down in the depths of the main valley glides the strong river, unconscious'.[36] Ruskin is achingly aware of how the two landscapes, the wet and the dry, are linked by underground runnels and trickles. He makes sense of these interconnected ecosystems by close looking, coupled with a desire to understand the structure of the earth, which he has carried with him since he was a boy.

Ruskin not only sees, but he also imagines what can be seen, if we burrow down, or soar skywards. In the same way that he urges Turner to recreate what would be a true vision of the Garden of the Hesperides, he leads us into impossible places, but with his clarity of sight still intact. In an extraordinary passage in *The Stones of Venice*, he tries to visualise the flight of a swallow across Europe, from the Mediterranean to the Arctic Circle. Even today, when we are accustomed to seeing the earth from the air as we cruise at 30,000 feet, this is a breathtaking view of his portion of the world. It encompasses all the lands he had ever seen, and many he could only imagine, in vibrant colour and sensation. He wrote repeatedly in *The Stones of Venice* about the pleasure of the eye. This pleasure in loveliness was not mere sensuality – it was the combination of sight and association. In this passage

38

he allowed his eye and his mind to weave a set of images, to explain how the architectures of northern and southern Europe grew out of their surroundings. It is worth quoting at length, and to imagine him reading it aloud:

We know that gentians grow on the Alps, and olives on the Apennines; but we do not enough conceive for ourselves that variegated mosaic of the world's surface which a bird sees in its migration, that difference between the district of the gentian and of the olive which the stork and the swallow see far off, as they lean upon the sirocco wind. Let us, for a moment, try to raise ourselves even above the level of their flight, and imagine the Mediterranean lying beneath us like an irregular lake, and all its ancient promontories sleeping in the sun: here and there an angry spot of thunder, a grey stain of storm, moving upon the burning field; and here and there a fixed wreath of white volcano smoke, surrounded by its circle of ashes; but for the most part a great peacefulness of light, Syria and Greece, Italy and Spain, laid like pieces of a golden pavement into the sea-blue, chased, as we stoop nearer to them, with bossy beaten work of mountain chains, and glowing softly with terraced gardens, and flowers heavy with frankincense, mixed among masses of laurel and orange and plumy palm, that abate with their grey-green shadows the burning of the marble rocks, and of the ledges of porphyry sloping under lucent sand. Then let us pass farther towards the north, until we see the orient colours change gradually into a vast belt of rainy green, where the pastures of Switzerland, and poplar valleys of France, and dark forests of the Danube and Carpathians stretch from the mouths of the Loire to those of the Volga, seen through clefts in grey swirls of rain-cloud and flaky veils of the mist of the brooks, spreading low along the pasture lands: and then, farther north still, to see the earth heave into mighty masses of leaden rock and heathy moor, bordering with a broad waste of gloomy purple that belt of field and wood, and splintering into irregular and grisly islands amidst the northern seas, beaten by storm, and chilled by ice-drift, and tormented by furious pulses of contending tide, until the roots of the last forests fail from among the hill ravines, and the hunger of the north wind bites their peaks into barrenness; and at last, the wall of ice, durable like iron, sets, deathlike, its white teeth against us out of the polar twilight.'[37]

It is deliberately ostentatious and heady in its phrasing. This is Ruskin at his most ebullient. But it is not mere showing-off. He is offering us a new insight into the interconnectedness of style, materials and the landscape, through an unexpected point of view. The gorgeous colours, the shifting surfaces of marble, meadow and ice, will remain with us, long after we close his book.

Ruskin challenges us in every chapter, every lecture. How perceptive are we? He urges us to train ourselves to be visually literate. He could not have known how needful this would be in the postmodern environment, where we take visual hits constantly. We have to learn to discriminate. Being aware of how we see the world is intimately bound up with the other things that mattered to Ruskin: learning to draw; taking our time as we stop to look; working out the relationships between a building and the people who built it and used it; being aware of our small place in a vast, ancient world; being thankful but questioning the status quo; stretching ourselves to imagine how it might be. All these ways of being in the world are enhanced by looking more closely.

Chapter 2
Drawing

Study of the Sea-horse of Venice

A patch of grass

Weeds and rough grass beneath my bare feet. I am sitting out after breakfast on a sheltered step already warmed by the sun of Aquitaine. I have been trying to get the measure of the hazy landscape of vineyards and far-off chateaux. But it is hard to concentrate, before the coffee kicks in, so I look down instead at the patch of untended earth in front of me. Not much there really, a bit of green and yellow. But then Ruskin catches me unawares, with a memory of a passage I read last night. As a child, he said,

> when the weather was fine, my time [in the garden] was passed chiefly in . . . close watching of the ways of plants. I had not the smallest taste for growing them, or taking care of them, any more than for taking care of the birds, or the trees, or the sky, or the sea. My whole time passed in staring at them, or into them.[38]

What would he make of this little space at my feet? I lean forward and notice that there are two different yellow flowers; one is tiny and clustered like clover, the other seems to be a sort of dandelion. Then there is a collection of small silvery star-like leaves, and just beyond them, cupped leaves edged with pink. Almost under my feet, I find a few miniature orange-red petals. A winding plant, with leaves shaped like spears, curves around a blade of grass. Wild strawberries beside me. Leggy daisies, with stalks too fine for daisy chains. Fragile poppies. Small succulents with hot pink flowers. I lift my eyes a little higher, taking in the swaying lavender, visited by strange moths that hover like hummingbirds, and fat black bees. If Ruskin were here, surely he would be able to tell me what these plants or insects are, and then paint word pictures with their Latin and French and English names. He would explain how they were woven into old stories or decorated the borders of manuscripts.

I want to remember these small, colourful treasures. I try to take a couple of photos, but they can't refine and focus. The shapes overlap, the sheen is lost, the greens all merge. It is no substitute for close looking. There is one way to make sure that these details are preserved. Ruskin would get out his pencil and sketchbook, and make quick visual notes, and write the colours in the corner. He would capture the outlines of leaves, and their differences in scale and smoothness. He had trained his eyes and hand precisely for this purpose.

The drawing master

Ruskin started drawing when he was little. He liked to copy maps and the illustrations in his book of Grimm's fairy stories. He knew that he 'could literally draw nothing, not a cat, not a mouse, not a boat, not a bush, "out of my head,"' but when he was copying, he worked with 'incredible, exactness'.[39]

Even as an adult, Ruskin never really moved on from this exactness. Yet his drawings and watercolours reveal an intense love of living things and buildings, carefully selected, intimately seen. He rarely drew people, except himself, and these self-portraits are not flattering. They are more hesitant than his usual sketches, the pencil line wavering over the contours of his face. He made sure that his necktie matched the blue of his eyes, mixing the correct shade in his dish of watercolours. (Ruskin was not vain but he always dressed with precision, and his cravat was invariably soft blue, exactly like his eyes.)

He sometimes copied figures from paintings that mattered to him; he particularly loved Carpaccio's sleeping *St Ursula* in Venice, and the tomb sculpture of *Ilaria del Carretto*, carved by Jacopo della Quercia after her death in 1405. But these were symbolic echoes of the only other face, apart from his own, that he drew obsessively – little Rose La Touche. He had come to know her, first as her drawing master, then as an engaging letter writer. He hoped one day, perhaps, to be her loving husband. Drawing, writing, caring, overlapped in the sad story of their romance.

In the Ruskin Library in Lancaster, there are four small drawings of a girl. These are, some might say, the central images of his life, the vision of perfect innocent beauty that haunted him from his late thirties until his death. Rose was a fair child, her hair touched with gold, whom Ruskin grew to love. His portraits of her begin with a careful water-colour study made when she was about twelve. Later we find a pale pencil sketch of a young woman with wild hair flaming across her pillow. In most of the pictures her eyes are lowered, her face turned away. But in this last drawing, Rose looks directly at Ruskin, with big dark eyes. They both knew she was dying.

She was a 'fiery little thing' when she met Ruskin, but over the years their strange friendship had become troubled and twisted. From her late teens Rose was often ill, perhaps with anorexia, certainly with anxiety and extreme religiosity. Ruskin hoped to marry her when she turned eighteen. However, her parents objected, and Rose was not clear in her own mind. The uncertainties and silences undermined Ruskin's own sanity. Her death in 1875 was one of the triggers for his mental health crises. He never fully recovered. For the rest of his life, his writings and drawings were filled with memories of a girl who never grew up: every sketch he made of a wild rose or a primrose was a homage to her. Even the titles of his books, particularly *Proserpina (studies of wayside*

48

flowers while the air was yet pure), written in the immediate aftermath of her loss, had a rose hidden at its heart.

Ruskin had become Rose's drawing master in the New Year of 1858, when she was nine years old. Her mother sought him out because she thought Ruskin was 'the only sound teacher in Art'.[40] And so he sat beside little Rose, guiding her hand. He sometimes took on a few private pupils and had just published a step-by-step manual, *The Elements of Drawing in three letters to beginners*. This hugely popular book was partly based on his own classes at the Working Men's College, in Red Lion Square, Holborn, where he taught alongside the Pre-Raphaelite painter Rossetti. It also grew out of recent correspondence with a young lady who was unable to attend these classes. Ruskin was becoming conscious that women were at a disadvantage when it came to art education. (When he was later appointed Slade Professor at Oxford, he made a point of giving his lectures to the male undergraduates, and then repeating them 'for the bonnets'.)

Ruskin used his own memories of childhood to lay the groundwork. He said that children should be given drawing materials and encouraged to 'scrawl at [their] own free will', rather than being judged or praised by their parents. They should have watercolour paints, and a storybook with 'good woodcuts' to enjoy. (Although, with a nod to his own airless upbringing, Ruskin insisted that if they scribbled on their picture books or daubed with their colours, the paintbox should be put out of reach).

As soon as possible, Ruskin suggested that a child should start to draw 'the things it can see and likes, – birds, or butterflies, or flowers, or fruit'.[41] In their early teens, children could begin to work from prints and magazine illustrations, to discover how artists reproduce the round world in flat colour and line. Again, his choices were very personal. Look at Turner's images in a volume of poems about Italy. (This book had been the birthday gift that opened Ruskin's eyes to Turner, and turned his attention to art and nature.) Look at Dürer. Even trying to copy 'now and then a quarter of an inch square or so' of Dürer's print of *Melancholia*, or a bushy corner from *The Flight into Egypt*, would help us to understand how 'every one of his lines is firm, deliberate and accurately descriptive'.[42] If you can't afford your own Dürer engraving, find a photograph of the print instead. At a pinch, he says, you could buy a couple of back issues of *Punch*, and work from the woodcuts.

It is at this point that modern readers feel most out of touch with Ruskin. How many of us can afford one of Dürer's wood engravings or a single plate from Turner's *Liber Studiorum*? He was so at home with Dürer that he was quite happy to lend engravings to an aspiring artist like Elizabeth Siddal.[43] Access to these extraordinary things seemed every-day to him.

And yet, we have the kind of detailed colour photographic reproductions that he would never have dreamt of. Even better than this, nearly all of us can see these works first hand in our art galleries. For free. If we live within striking distance of London or Oxford, Manchester, Sheffield or Glasgow, we can visit the print rooms of our city art collections. We might have to book a couple of days in advance. We might need to leave our bags in the cloakroom and use a pencil. But these places are open to all. We don't need to be students or specialists. We just need to ask. So we can get up close to *Melancholia*, or see the glorious swirling snowscapes of Turner's *Italy*. This is a Victorian legacy to our modern cities. Philanthropists including Ruskin donated their rich collections for us all to study and explore. As we will see, he was particularly keen to donate works to Sheffield for the benefit of the metalworkers and artisans of the city. The Ruskin Collection is still there, at the heart of the Millennium Galleries. Like other wealthy patrons, he wanted us to share his good fortune, and enjoy our adventures in art.[44]

Sky, tree, stone

The Elements of Drawing still have a lot to teach us. To start with, Ruskin believes that everyone can draw usefully, so long as they are prepared to practise. He claims that 'I have never yet, in the experiments I have made, met with a person who could not learn to draw at all' and that it is no different from learning French or maths. Drawing is less demanding than learning to play the piano well – something that many of his young female readers would already have mastered, even though Ruskin estimated that 'it takes three or four years of practice, giving three or four hours a day, to acquire even ordinary command over the keys of a piano'. He expects us to be diligent. But with 'an hour's practice a day for six months', he believes you can gain 'sufficient power of drawing faithfully whatever you want to draw, and a good judgment, up to a certain point, of other people's work'.[45]

And this is the reason for writing his book. Ruskin explains why it is good to draw. He is clear that the aim of drawing is not to make us less dreary at dinner parties, or to entertain us when we're bored. It is not to make bold, expressive pictures with sparkle and swagger. Drawing is a useful skill that makes us see more clearly. It allows us to record the things that matter to us, and to recognise good work when we find it.

We begin, as we always do with Ruskin, by stepping outside: 'I would rather teach drawing that my pupils may learn to love Nature,' he explained, 'than teach the looking at Nature that they may learn to draw.'[46] In his first lesson, we think about composing a view, even a very ordinary view, by looking through a pane of glass or an empty picture frame. How does our impression of the landscape change when we focus on one particular part of it? And then he gives us the tools to 'to set down clearly, and usefully, records of such things as cannot be described in words'.[47]

Start with the sky: 'any narrow space of evening sky, that you can usually see, between the boughs of a tree, or between two chimneys, or through the corner of a pane in the window you like best to sit at.'[48] (He recognises that most of us are cooped up in towns, with narrow gardens if we are lucky.) The early lessons help us to work with our materials, to create soft, accurate lines with our pens, and quiet, even tints with our watercolours. Avoid the flourish and the slapdash. The best work is always controlled. At twilight, look carefully at the shades of grey or purple or blue in the darkening sky, and 'try to gradate a little space of white paper as evenly as that is gradated – as *tenderly*'.[49] He often asks us to work tenderly and delicately. Ruskin encourages us to treat our subjects with love, as if they feel the strokes of our brush. And if we get tired and impatient, look up, look again at the sky, and see the beauty there – that is why we bother.

The idea of making a colour chart, filled with small squares of paint, began when Ruskin was a boy. He wanted to be sure of the exact colour of the sky, to make his observations about the weather and cloud patterns. So he painted a cyanometer – a small piece of card, shaded with lighter and darker cobalt blues – which he carried with him on his travels so he could hold it up and match it against the colour of the heavens.[50] Truth and beauty are inseparable in his eyes.

The next task is to look at a tree. 'Choose any tree that you think pretty, which is nearly bare of leaves, and which you can see against the sky, or against a pale wall'.[51] The boughs will look dark against the lighter background, but the contrast shouldn't be too strong as it will dazzle or glint. This is a lesson for a grey day. Ruskin asks us to follow the lines of the branches as they grow up and out. 'Consider them as so many dark rivers,' he says, 'to be laid down in a map with absolute accuracy.' Look at the positive and negative spaces, the white in between as much as the dark solids. Copy them, make a record of how they appear here and now, before the sun comes out again, or the wind catches them. And 'do not take any trouble about the little twigs, which look like a confused network or mist';[52] they will come later. For now we are concentrating on the essentials.

When you have mapped the tree, go out and find a stone. Not too shiny, quite rounded or oval, whitish or brownish, with cracks and blemishes and signs of where it has been, like any other stone. Use a pencil and look at the curve of its surface. Make it visible on the page through the fall of light, the ins and outs of its form. The process of building up the three dimensions through shading and hatching is subtle and, yes, it is slow. Don't draw the outline first. The natural world is not made of edges, but of masses and tints. Man-made things might be circumscribed with clear silhouettes, but that is not what Ruskin wants us to look at. He is not training us to design for industry. There are other schools, other teachers for that. He is training us to see and to record.

Ruskin expects us to get to know our stone. He uses it to teach us about drawing rocky landscapes and river valleys: 'cracks or fissures of any kind ... are never expressible by single black lines ... A crack must always have its complete system of light and shade, however small its scale. It is in reality a little ravine, with a dark or shady side, and light or

54

sunny side.'[53] He suggests we make a small hole in a piece of card and hold it up in front of our 'stone antagonist'. Looking through this hole, we notice the various colours and markings more clearly. We clear our view of distractions.

'Now if you can draw that stone, you can draw anything; I mean, anything that is drawable.' Ruskin has offered us a key to the visible world. There are things that can be drawn. There are some that can be seen and enjoyed, but 'cannot be drawn at all, only the idea of them more or less suggested' like sea foam. But if we can build up the sensation of looking at the fall of light on a solid object, like the stone, and do it, as Ruskin says, 'rightly', then

> everything within reach of art is also within yours. For all drawing depends, primarily, on your power of representing Roundness. If you can once do that, all the rest is easy and straightforward; if you cannot do that, nothing else that you may be able to do will be of any use. For Nature is all made up of roundnesses; not the roundness of perfect globes, but of variously curved sur-faces. Boughs are rounded, leaves are rounded, stones are rounded, clouds are rounded, cheeks are rounded, and curls are rounded: there is no more flatness in the natural world than there is vacancy.[54]

These rounded things are also better drawn than described in words. We can be more exact about their proportions, textures and colours. There is precision in pencil and paint. Ruskin's writings can bring us closer to understanding the details of a flower or an Alpine view than most. But even he falls short, as he cannot show us everything simultaneously on the page, as he might in a drawing.

Ruskin did not always find drawing easy himself. He also had to make the effort to concentrate. One of the most revealing passages in his autobiography shows the effectiveness of drawing, in giving us back the power to appreciate the obvious.

Take a tree, beside a path, on a hot afternoon. Ruskin came across it when he was on holiday. He had been underwhelmed by the sights of Fontainebleau, and was tired and cross. He had developed a 'savage dislike of palaces and straight gravel walks'. So he stopped, sat down and closed his eyes, but couldn't rest. There was a small aspen tree, alone against the blue sky. He pulled paper and pencil from a pocket, out of habit.

> Languidly, but not idly, I began to draw it; and as I drew, the languor passed away: the beautiful lines insisted on being traced, – without weariness. More and more beautiful they became, as each rose out of the rest, and took its place in the air. With wonder increasing every instant, I saw that they 'composed' themselves, by finer laws than any known of men. At last, the tree was there, and everything that I had thought before about trees, nowhere.[55]

Ruskin discovered that the act of drawing was transformative. It restored his curiosity, and his sense of place and possibilities. He never forgot that tree or how it made him feel. He realised 'that all the trees of the wood (for I saw surely that my little aspen was only one of their millions) should be beautiful', more beautiful than Gothic tracery, or embroidery, or a magnificent painting. It gave him, as he remembered, 'an insight into a new silvan world'. It was no longer enough to think and write about pictures. He became acutely aware of the links between living, moving things. 'The woods, which I had only looked on as wilderness, fulfilled I then saw, in their beauty, the same laws which guided the clouds, divided the light, and balanced the wave.'[56] Trees, clouds, waves were all delightful and interrelated. He remembered this as a revelation, changing the way he thought. It helped him to develop his vocation as a critic, and to show the world what he had seen.

'Beautiful things that pass away'

So what? Why should we care about Ruskin's day out in France, and his transcendent excitement about a tree? Why bother to carry a card in your bag painted in different shades of blue? Why does the colour of the sky matter? Or the shape of a tree, and the way it dances in a breeze? Ruskin had leisure and money and nothing better to do than sit and draw. We're busy. We can't just cloud-watch.

But Ruskin cloud-watched every day. It was not just idle curiosity. It meant that he noticed climate change caused by industrial pollution. He was not the only person in his generation to fear the impact of industrialisation on the landscape. John Stuart Mill, for example, prophesied a world 'with nothing left . . . every flowery waste or natural pasture ploughed up, all quadrupeds or birds which are not domesticated for man's use exterminated as his rivals for food, every hedgerow or superfluous tree rooted out, and scarcely a place left where a wild shrub or flower could grow without being eradicated as a weed in the name of improved agriculture'.[57] This was a culture which indulged in apocalyptic fears – of the aging of the earth, or the dying of the sun; the stuff of H.G. Wells's science fiction, and anxious sermons in Anglo-Catholic pulpits.

Ruskin, however, looked beyond the hyperbole, to something grounded in visual truth. He was one of the very first observers to give prophetic warning of devastating smog and contaminated waterways. He wanted to understand the complex connections between weather and landscape, how climate interacted with architecture and geology. He made notes and sketches, and understood the passage of sun and rain. He saw how the weather worked. He noticed when it changed.

One of the virtues of drawing was to 'obtain quicker perceptions of the beauty of the natural world'. Another was to 'preserve something like a true image of beautiful things that pass away, or which you must yourself leave'.[58] Transient beauty – drifting clouds, swift waters, falling petals – are remembered accurately in his watercolours. The changing seasons are anticipated from year to year as he compares the dates in his diaries, or illustrations in letters. And he knows when something is wrong. He spots abnormal patterns: odd clouds, unseasonal storms, strangely dark sunsets or delayed sunrises.

He had often encouraged his audiences to draw the dawn, and some of his own colour notes are still kept in the Ashmolean Museum. 'Rise early,' he said, 'always watch the sunrise, and the way the clouds break from the dawn.'[59] He worked on blue-grey paper, catching the mare's tails in their crimson and purple glory before they were lost. He loved to paint in the evenings too. His lecture diagrams showed 'one of the last pure sunsets' he ever saw, in 1876: 'the sort of thing Turner and I used to have to look at.'[60]

Turner was his talisman, as the ideal painter of the world outside the window. Ruskin suggested that his readers should 'watch for the next barred sunrise' and then pick up a copy of Turner's illustrated poems of *Italy* to test the pictures 'by nature's own clouds'. Telling the truth about the visible world was one of Turner's gifts. Ruskin recognised that these pictures could be used as a measure of beauty, and of disruption, particularly in the years since Turner's death in 1851. He missed the golden glow of Turner's evening skies and the clear colours of his early-morning studies. Ruskin remembered twilight scenes from his early travels, when 'a broad field of cloud is advancing ... but there is no power in them to pollute the sky beyond and above them: they do not darken the air, nor defile it ... their edges are burnished by the sun'.[61]

Ruskin's observations were scientific as well as aesthetic. The results were disturbing. In 1871 he began to record his concerns about a change in the atmosphere. 'It is the first of July,' he wrote,

> and I sit down to write by the dismallest light that ever yet I wrote by ... For the sky is covered with grey cloud; – not rain-cloud, but a dry black veil, which no ray of sunshine can pierce; partly diffused in mist, feeble mist ... And everywhere the leaves of the trees are shaking fitfully ... to show the passing to and fro of a strange, bitter, blighting wind.[62]

He had become aware of a problem in the spring, with a 'changelessly sullen April, through despondent May, and darkened June'. 'It is a new thing to me,' he wrote, 'and a very dreadful one.' He kept watch. It did not pass, and year after year became worse. In 1884, he was sure that this was a permanent change. His lecture, *The Storm-Cloud of the Nineteenth Century* is the result of his constant, careful looking. He was furious and eloquent. He tried to bring it home to his audience using extra-large painted diagrams of massed clouds in motion: 'no colours that can be fixed in earth,' he wrote, 'can ever represent to you the lustre' of the clouds he had seen in his younger days, 'golden and ruby ... Tyrian crimson and Byzantine purple ... vermilion against green blue'. Now it looked as they were 'made of poisonous smoke; very possibly it may be: there are at least two hundred furnace chimneys in a square of two miles on every side of me. But mere smoke would not blow to and fro in that wild way. It looks more to me as if it were made of dead men's souls.'[63]

Storm-cloud and plague wind. 'Blanched Sun, – blighted grass, – blinded man'. Dead men's souls. Of course, most listeners were sceptical. Ruskin acknowledged that his concerns were dismissed in the press as 'imaginary, or insane'. But he insisted that he knew what he was talking about. Ruskin explained that until the 1860s, 'when weather was fine, it was luxuriously fine; when it was bad ... it had its fit of temper and was done with it – it didn't sulk for three months without letting you see the sun.' He talked of the clouds of beneficent rain, 'capable also of the most exquisite colouring', and the rainbows that formed as they cleared. He spoke lovingly of thunderclouds, 'always majestic, often dazzlingly beautiful'.[64] But now, above Brantwood, he saw weather systems that were new and troubling:

all sky interwoven with muslin and netting of divinest cirri cloud, over infinite shoals and sands of mackerel cloud; but all flying, failing, melting – re-appearing –

61

twisting and intertwisting – faster than eye could follow ... ending in two great ranks of storm-cloud ...
with long locks and tresses ... northward in a clear
sky against a black monster cloud ... falling forward
like a gloomy and slow avalanche and melting, as it
was torn down or dragged, into nothingness. I believe
these swift and mocking clouds and colours are only
between storms. They are assuredly new in Heaven, so
far as my life reaches. I never saw a single example of
them till after 1870.[65]

Scientific language seemed inadequate to describe these
phenomena. Ruskin used metaphors and allusions; his
clouds are dragons, tigers or dolphins. Other observers, like
Professor Tyndall, a pioneering mountain climber, geologist
and physicist, wrote of cloud behaviour in terms of waves
and vibrations. Ruskin rounded on him: 'Do you suppose a
water-wave is like a harpstring? ... You see a field of corn
undulating as if it was water, – it is different from the flag ...
and yet, is no more like the undulation of the sea, than the
shaking of an aspen leaf.'[66] These inaccuracies and incon-
sistencies in vocabulary made it all the more necessary to
record what he saw in drawings and diagrams. He needed
to be able to answer his critics by pointing to particulars in
his sketchbooks and diaries.

When Ruskin tried to explain why these changes were
happening, he found it hard. The strange sunsets of the

mid-1880s were almost certainly caused by the massive explosions on the Indonesian island of Krakatoa in August 1883. Four catastrophic eruptions sent volcanic material – dust plumes and gases – seventeen miles into the atmosphere. Over 36,000 people were killed by the falling pumice, or subsequent tsunamis. And the skies darkened – in America and Europe as well as in Asia. The moon looked green or blue or lavender-coloured. Sometimes it seemed like the horizon was on fire. Ruskin was extremely interested in volcanoes and referred to an earlier eruption in 1877 in his work, *Deucalion*, published in 1883. But he had noted a deterioration in the weather from the early 1870s, so it must be more than this.

Ruskin pointed to the pollution of the industrialising cities around the north-west of England. The factory chimneys of Manchester, Liverpool and Lancaster were undoubtedly filling the air with filth. Yet the smoke alone could not account for 'the most hellish – frantic, terrific wind I've ever listened to, the climax of two days and nights perpetual black with sleet', such as he experienced at Brantwood in January 1878.[67] He had often travelled in the Lakes with his family before he moved there after his father's death, so he knew that the weather was unpredictable and often stormy. He sometimes recorded weather that came across the water as it used to, with 'soft flaky raincloud moving slowly – showing hills through rents in the old way', but this only reinforced 'how totally prevalent the plague cloud, sooty and furious, has been – for this is quite wonderful and lovely to me'.[68]

In his 'Storm-Cloud' lecture Ruskin claimed that the signs in the sky were caused by blasphemy – by Britain turning away from God's teachings. What are we to make of this now? Should we just dismiss Ruskin's observations and anxieties because, after all the science and visual studies, he cannot escape the religious framework of his thinking? He was wrestling with his Christian upbringing, like many of his generation. His own fears that he was falling away from faith made him question where this might lead. If he and his contemporaries no longer followed God's laws, maybe this was the result?

Perhaps we can reword his argument. In Ruskin's eyes, the natural world was God's creation. Again and again he writes of God breathing life into plants and animals, mountains and rivers. For him, our relationship with and understanding of these things comes from God: he encourages his readers to hope for 'all the knowledge of the waters and the earth that God meant for you'.[69]

Put another way, it is the job and the joy of mankind to look after the earth, its waters and its creatures. But by refusing to honour and care for nature, by plundering and polluting, by wasting and littering, modern men and women indeed behave as if there is no life after their death, no need to worry about anything bigger than their own immediate desires. Ruskin did not need God to tell him that the consequences of squandering the earth's resources would be disastrous. He could see the fragile webs that connected meadow flowers with pollinating insects and sources of clear water and clean air. If we trample and muddy them we will alter the ecosystems that he drew so tenderly. His gaze moved constantly from the small-scale to the large, from the individual plant to the species and its environment. He could see the bigger picture. He showed us how we have failed in our stewardship.

Ruskin also knew that darkening skies overhead had an impact on our own inner vision. We lose sight of the things that lift our spirits, and we feel bereft. He experienced prolonged and devastating depression and mental instability, beginning in the mid-1870s. It was triggered by grief at the death of his parents and Rose. But it was also directly connected with his fears about the 'storm-cloud' and hellish wind. He noted in his diary for 11 February 1881, 'some dim blue sky, with scudding cloud, but getting darker, and I am utterly horror-struck and hopeless about the weather. The plague wind now *constant* and the sun virtually extinguished'. Ten days later, he was dreadfully ill again, with 'a breakdown of the brain'.[70] He could not draw. His words dried up. He smashed the glass in his bedroom window. He had seen it coming, but could not avert the storm.

Chapter 3
Building

The Southern Porch of Saint Wulfram, Abbeville

The stones of Abbeville

Sitting in a café in Picardy, Ruskin wrote to his father: 'I have been doing my best to draw the Cathedral porch; but alas, it is not so easily done. I seem born to conceive what I cannot execute ... and mourn over what I cannot save.' He was watching the medieval cathedrals and houses disappearing before his eyes. 'In twenty years it is plain that not a vestige of Abbeville, or indeed of any old French town, will be left.'[71]

I visited Abbeville in May this year. He was right. Ruskin had been outraged by the vandalism of restoration in the 1840s. When he was there, workmen were 'knocking down the time-worn black with age pinnacles, and sticking up in their place new stone ones to be carved at some future time.'[72] Blank blocks were replacing the intricate crockets around the door frames. Ruskin felt so desperate that he threatened to knock the men off their scaffolding. What would he have said now about the stump of the cathedral and the graceless shopping precinct built in its shadow? How could he have borne the devastation of this medieval masterpiece in the bombardments of 1940? Time, restoration, war and soulless reconstruction have undone the Flamboyant Gothic that Ruskin sat and studied. At least we have his words and pictures to show us how glorious it used to be.

Ruskin's efforts of concentrated looking, and the records he made, enabled him to reconstruct the history of buildings in Britain and across Europe. When he was travelling, he would set out straight after breakfast with his notebooks and tape measures, and sketch old houses and churches for six hours a day. He drew their details, adding notes in the margin. He copied the colours of their marbles and mosaics with his paints. He set up tripods and captured their light and shade, the ivy clinging to their surfaces, with daguerreotype photography. He organised teams to create plaster casts of the most delicate carved capitals and traceries. He climbed ladders, stuck his head out of windows, cajoled, protested and preserved. He loved buildings.

This affection was partly a heartfelt reaction to the visual delight of standing in front of buildings like Abbeville or Rouen cathedrals. Ruskin was at times embarrassed by his 'love of all sorts of filigree and embroidery, from hoarfrost to the high clouds'. He said that 'the intricacies of virgin silver, of arborescent gold, the weaving of birds'-nests, the netting of lace, the basket capitals of Byzantium, and most of all the tabernacle work of the French flamboyant school' wove a charm over him that was hard to break.[73] The swelling and dipping of the outlines. The sense of weightlessness and confidence carried up through the buttresses and into the soaring spires, defying gravity. Rock transformed into tendrils. The designs were constantly surprising. And it was not just the sensation of looking from the outside. Ruskin also felt energised and exultant inside the medieval churches of France.

Very specifically, on 5 June 1835 as a sixteen-year-old, he first stepped into St Wulfran's in Abbeville. He remembered it clearly, fifty years later. Like his epiphany in the Alps, he suddenly saw the world knit together. Ruskin began to understand how our surroundings and our love of the past flow into our potential for happiness, offering 'healthy labour and joy'. What he found in Abbeville was a combination of art, religion and life 'in perfect harmony'. And he felt this was because he could walk into and around the church, unhindered.

He had been brought up with his mother's Evangelical piety weighing heavy on him. His London church sucked the ecstasy and creativity out of worship. It concentrated on words, especially Bible reading and sermons, rather than the sense of sight – which was the way to Ruskin's heart. His exposure to the Roman Catholic traditions in France opened up an alternative approach to God. He had been schooled to respect and dread Sundays. At home, the Sabbath meant tedious godly books and long services in wooden pews. Here in France, it seemed 'there were no dead six days and dismal seventh'. It seemed almost sinful to take such delight in church. Yet in Abbeville, he could spend his days in 'sculptured churches; there was no beadle to lock me out of them ... I might haunt them, fancying myself a ghost; peep round their pillars ... kneel in them, and scandalize nobody; draw in them, and disturb none'. As he said, 'My most intense happinesses have of course been among mountains. But for cheerful, unalloyed, unwearying pleasure, the getting in sight of Abbeville on a fine summer afternoon ... and rushing down the street to see St. Wulfran again before the sun was off the towers, are things to cherish the past for, – to the end.'[74]

So, as I stood in front of the locked west doors of Abbeville in the spring sunshine, it felt as if Ruskin had brought me there. But I could rejoice with him only in memory. It was sad to see the great triple-arched porch overlooked by the concrete low-rise flats and shops, their doors also shut. This sense of being excluded is hard to bear. Ruskin loved to explore and experience a building in all dimensions, thinking back across time, as well as up and out. In his writings he slowly walks with us around the outside walls, pointing out the parts he likes best, then in through the wooden doors to the sudden darkness. As our eyes become attuned to the fall of light through the high windows, we follow him along the aisles, stopping at the side chapels, moving towards the east end.

Flamboyant

In some of Ruskin's favourite churches, this is still possible. Rouen cathedral is wonderfully accessible, from all angles. We can open a small door under the south tower, and walk through. No one will stop us, no stewards with official lanyards, no compulsory guided tour. This is a rare treat.

In Rouen we can explore freely: here is the tomb of Richard the Lionheart near the high altar; beyond it, the thirteenth-century glass glowing blue and red, signed by Clement of Chartres. When we have had our fill of looking here, we head back outside, and around the corner. We find the threshold of a large gateway down a side street, and step in to see the northern transept porch, which meant so much to Ruskin. It was a highpoint of Flamboyant architecture, when the shaped stone seemed to flame like fire rising from a blazing torch (or *flambeau*). He wrote of this carved gable as a 'great watershed of Gothic art'.

For Ruskin, these carvings represented a shift in the way builders thought about materials. Here, he said, 'the traceries had *caught the eye* of the architect'. Until that moment, 'his eye had been on the openings only, on the stars of light. He did not care about the stone'. After this, 'change was like a low breeze', making the tracery tremble. 'It began to undulate like the threads of a cobweb lifted by the wind. It lost its essence as a structure of stone.' For a short while, Ruskin felt, this tension between flexibility and stoniness was full of potential. But when, in later Gothic, the carved outlines became more delicate, and 'the whole fragility, elasticity, and weight of the material are to the eye . . . denied', he became disillusioned. When two mouldings 'appear to pass through the other . . . [and] they melted into each other', this was the beginning of the end for Gothic art.[75]

Ruskin was outraged by this change in the treatment of stonework. His criticism was expressed in phrases that were personal and morally charged. This was 'treachery' and 'falsehood'. It seemed 'degrading'.[76] Why did it matter so much to him, this falling away from the 'radiant unity', the 'pause of the star', 'the great, pure, and perfect form of French Gothic'?[77] What was he scared of?

He seems to be frightened of two things. Firstly, this new direction in art rejects the idea of 'truth to materials'. Ruskin despairs when builders begin to manipulate stone as if it is pliable, 'as a silken cord'.[78] Truth to materials was one of the key messages of Ruskin's writings, throughout his life and beyond. As we have seen, it mattered that, when Turner painted rainstorms or rivers, the water appeared properly wet. It was the same in all the arts. Wood should look and act like wood, stone like stone. As he later explained in his lectures on *The Two Paths*, 'if you don't want the qualities of the substance you use, you ought to use some other substance', otherwise it 'can be only affectation and desire to display'. 'Glass, for instance, is eminently, in its nature, transparent. If you don't want transparency, let the glass alone.'[79] Make the most of the materials in front of you. Show your workings, he says. Don't cover solid wood with veneer, don't pretend pine is mahogany, or plastic is porcelain. Or that stone can penetrate stone. Don't lie.

Secondly, and closely related, is the suggestion of arrogance. In late Gothic buildings, he says, there is an extravagance, a focus on cleverness for its own sake, pushing a structure to its limits. Sometimes it is hard to see why this should be a fault. But what if we turn our attention to something nearer to home? What would Ruskin make of the recent spate of skyscrapers in London and Manchester that are wider at the top than at the base? What do we make of them? Deliberately disturbing, seeming ready to topple, defying our instinct for buildings to be rooted, they are the latest examples of architectural impudence. Beetham Tower (2006) with its slender cantilevered metal and glass construction, sways and hums loudly above Deansgate in high winds. Another top-heavy tower, built in 2014 at 20 Fenchurch Street, London, also has problems with the weather. Its curved surface acts as a mirror, intensifying the sunlight and creating hotspots in the street, up to 117° Celsius. This solar glare, and the wind-tunnel effect at the foot of the tower, mean that the architects have failed to factor in the arbitrary or the elemental. They have forgotten how nature interacts with the city. This forgetfulness of the environment suggests that, as a society, we cannot think of anything more important than ourselves. We have lost sight of our little space on the earth, compared with the great expanse of clouds above and the winds that move them.

For Ruskin, his concern with arrogance and truth always intersected with religious anxiety. He seemed to see architects in the fifteenth century turning away from God and refocusing on themselves. They developed more self-confidence and swagger. This coincided with the rebirth of classical learning, of the Renaissance. And in classical terms, man becomes the measure of all things, rather than heaven and its angels. For a Renaissance artist like Leonardo da Vinci, it seemed obvious that man's body should be the ideal form, making geometry visible, standing firm within a drawn square or circle. But Ruskin looked at the world as the medieval poet Dante did, with God's love at the centre: 'Love that moves the sun and the other stars'.[80]

In Ruskin's criticism, the shift from God-centred to man-centred architecture was directly linked to the Renaissance and the Roman Catholic Counter-Reformation. He saw these two great cultural movements as a double-pronged attack on the values he held dear. He never shook off his Protestant prejudices. They coloured his criticism at every stage. His arguments were often contradictory and unsustainable, and they can make it hard for us to take his lecturing seriously. But at a fundamental level he felt at home in the world before 1500: before Raphael and Michelangelo; before Luther and Henry VIII; before people had to choose between a whitewashed box of a church, its glass and statues smashed by iconoclasts, or Bernini's grandiose designs for St Peter's in Rome; before Western Christendom was torn apart. Ruskin tried to spot the signs of it in the buildings he studied and cared for. Did this carving give a warning? Was this architect starting to feel smug and flashy? Where would this tracery fit into Ruskin's scheme of a decline into decadence?

It was not just about pointed or rounded arches. Or gargoyles versus cupids. To Ruskin, the differences in scale, decoration or atmosphere between Rouen cathedral and St Peter's expressed something essential about the way patrons thought about their relationship with their architects and workers. And the natural world. And the history of ancient Greece and Rome. And ultimately their relationship with God.

Sometimes the enthusiasm and invective of his writing obscures the most important outcomes. We have to remind ourselves that his close reading of medieval architecture bore fruit. Ruskin was a campaigner. He was a pioneer in speaking out, and urging his audiences to treat the built environment as a gift from the past. It mattered that the evidence of the stones should not be lost. As one of the founders of the Society of the Protection of Ancient Buildings (SPAB), he took practical steps to preserve the beautiful and the old. He invested in the Guild of St George. The guild took care of the plaster casts that he had collected, so that details of carving might outlast the pollution and restoration of the nineteenth century. He could not rely on other people to take these steps. He could see what needed doing. Ruskin drew attention to the laziness or short-sightedness of modern architects. He refused to cut corners, or simply hope for the best. He believed that artists had a duty to keep these lovely things safe, at least in memory.

He had learnt from an earlier generation, particularly artists like Samuel Prout, and knew how much was already beyond his reach. Ruskin feared that his work, like Prout's, would one day 'be cherished with a melancholy gratitude, when the pillars of Venice shall lie mouldering in the salt shallows of her sea, and the stones of the goodly towers of Rouen have become ballast for the barges of the Seine'.[81]

This might sound like hyperbole. But the magnificent Norman abbey of Jumièges was still being ransacked as an easy source of dressed stone a very few years before Ruskin first visited France. And it was largely the actions of Ruskin, his friends and followers that stopped the devastating restoration of St Mark's, Venice. The south side of the basilica had already been stripped of its rain-polished marbles, and the mosaics and ancient stonework of the western facade were to be next. In 1879, the SPAB stepped in to protest about the planned work on the basilica. Their campaign was inspired by Ruskin's declaration in *The Lamp of Memory*: 'Do not let us talk then of restoration. The thing is a Lie from beginning to end ... Take proper care of your monuments.' He went on, 'They are not ours. They belong partly to those who built them, and partly to all the generations of mankind who are to follow us'.[82] He wrote to an Italian friend and fellow activist, Count Zorzi:

This catastrophe in Venice surpasses all in its miser-
ableness. St Mark's was the most rich in associations,
the most marvellous in beauty, the most perfect in
preservation . . . their mosaics especially were of such
exquisite intricacy of deep golden glow . . . [with] an
effect as of peacock's feathers in the sun, when their
green and purple glitters through and through with
light. But now they have the look of a peacock's feather
that has been dipped in white paint.[83]

Ruskin was devastated, and his despair compounded his mental instability. He apologised that he could not attend any
of the public meetings in defence of St Mark's: 'I am now
entirely unable to take part in exciting business, or even,
without grave danger, to allow my mind to dwell on the
subjects which, having once been dearest to it, are now the
sources of acutest pain.'[84]

He focused on creating 'such record as hand and heart
can make of the most precious building in Europe, standing
yet in the eyes of men and the sunshine of heaven'.[85] He
commissioned watercolours, plaster casts and photographs.
One of the largest paintings, by his assistant John Bunney,
shows the whole western front of the basilica. It records
most eloquently the insensitive attempts at restoration. The
city architects wanted to tidy up, to straighten, to unify,
the ancient building. They were cleaning the old delicately
coloured Greek marble facings, using acid and files. Some of

the stones were being replaced entirely. On the far edge of the picture, the new grey Italian marble had begun to wrap around the corner of the building. Subtle, polished golden surfaces were now dull and leaden. As Ruskin had said in 'The Lamp of Memory', a restored building is merely a corpse.

Ruskin wrote now, hopelessly, lovingly: he knew that his descriptions of St Mark's were 'occasionally read for the sound of them; and perhaps, when the building is destroyed, may be some day, with amazement, perceived to have been true'. St Mark's was a reliquary, a treasure house, a delight to the eye and the soul. 'Whatever remains' of the facade, he said, 'is perfect as on the day it was set in its place, mellowed and subdued only in colour by time, but white still, clearly white; and grey still, softly grey; its porphyry purple as an Orleans plum, and the serpentine as green as a greengage.'[86]

He could do nothing more. Mercifully he had done enough. The campaign gathered momentum and friends weighed in: artists and architects like Edward Burne-Jones, William Morris and Philip Webb, and admirers with more clout, including William Gladstone, all spoke out. In Italy, Count Zorzi continued to agitate and protest. Together they swayed opinion. And in March 1880 the scrubbing and removal of the ancient marbles and mosaics was stopped. Relief came too late for Ruskin. He only saw Venice once more, in the autumn of 1888, when he was, by all accounts 'very frail and somewhat vague in talk'.[87]

Ladders in Venice

Ruskin's affection for ancient buildings, and his determination to understand and care for them was unusual. Sometimes it seems that he was more sensitive to the stones than he was to the people around him. He had blind spots. When he was travelling around northern France in 1848 with his young wife Effie, she received news that her aunt Jessie had died of puerperal fever a month after her newborn son. Ruskin was more concerned about losing a day's work than in supporting his wife in her grief. And, even on good days, he simply did not understand why Effie had to trail around behind him. He could not see that she was stuck, unable to explore on her own without a companion.

When they visited Venice the following year, as he began work on *The Stones of Venice*, Effie made sure to bring a friend, so that Ruskin could concentrate on his work and she did not have to sit on a camping stool in the corner. He could turn his attention again to questions of tracery and pointed arches.

Ruskin tried to think himself back into the past. He wanted to understand the connections between faith, geography, climate, materials, systems of government, all the things that shaped a building. Sometimes he thought big, declaring 'the look of mountain brotherhood between the Cathedral and the Alp'. Sometimes he came right down to details. As Effie said in a letter to her brother, 'John is very busy in the Doge's

Palace all day, and as yet he has only drawn one capital of one pillar'.[88] Drawing all these elements together, he showed the interconnectedness of people and place. Hewn rock, cleft wood, baked brick. Great buildings are more than just shelter from the storm. They are expressions of hope, at once soaring and grounded. They have energy.

Ruskin saw and felt this. How could he make others see and feel it too? Until buildings could be explored and catalogued, it was impossible to understand who built them and why their shape and decoration changed from generation to generation. He needed to gather and sift, to work out what was distinctive. When he was preparing his first book on French buildings, he decided, 'I now know more about it than any English architect . . . I have not yet once succeeded in giving the *true* effect of a highly ornamental flamboyant niche, though I think I have come nearer it than most people.'[89] And during his researches in the Ducal Palace in Venice, he discovered that he was the first person to have looked properly at the window openings. Previous writers on the Gothic had been happy to stand in the square and guess. Ruskin badgered the custodians until they let him investigate at first hand. He had asked the librarian if there had ever been stone tracery in the windows:

Never, he said – there was not the slightest trace of it . . . Yesterday I . . . got the library steps and opened all the windows, one after another, round the palace.

82

I found the bases of the shafts of the old tracery ...
and finally, in a window at the back, of which I believe
not one of the people who have written on the place
know so much as the existence, one of its spiral shafts
left – capital and all.[90]

This thoroughness, this insistence of seeing for himself, was
the underpinning of all his work. He made slow progress. But
it enabled him to join the dots from place to place, column
by column. He came to know Venice by eye and by heart.

Throughout the winter of 1849–50, he worked his way
around the city, trying to piece together the story of Venice
through its buildings. The result was a compendium of
architectural drawings that showed the marvellous variety
and invention of the medieval builders. On one page (of
over 1,600 pages) of *The Stones of Venice*, he mapped out
the changing shapes of medieval windows. He showed how
they shifted from simple flat lintels with the development of
the cusp, a shaped stone that transformed the opening into
a leaf shape.[91] In the second volume, he carefully illustrated
thirty-seven different window forms: rounded, ogee, cusped,
doubled, pierced.[92] Here was so much ingenuity that had
been overlooked before.

What did he do with this knowledge? Ruskin used his
research to explain how and why these beautiful buildings
had been created. *The Stones of Venice* evolved into a narrative
of the rise and fall of an ideal society. It reads like a romance.

Ruskin had loved the city since he was sixteen; he called it an 'enchanted world'. He had been given a foretaste through his fascination with Turner and Byron. He recalled his 'rapture, on the morning that brought us in sight of Venice: and the black knot of gondolas in the canal of Mestre, more beautiful to me than a sunrise full of clouds all scarlet and gold ... marble walls rising out of the salt sea, with hosts of little brown crabs on them, and Titians inside'.[93] He was enthralled by the lavish complexity of the medieval minds and hands that he found there.

'The Nature of Gothic'

Ruskin drew together his ideas in one central chapter of *The Stones of Venice*. This chapter, 'The Nature of Gothic', lies at the heart of the book. Some say that it encapsulates Ruskin's way of looking at the world. The poet and designer William Morris would certainly agree. He said that this was 'one of the most important things written by the author, and in future days will be considered as one of the very few necessary and inevitable utterances of the century'. Morris, as ever, was more succinct than Ruskin. He was able to sum up the eighty-nine pages in one phrase: 'For the lesson which Ruskin here teaches us is that art is the expression of man's pleasure in labour'.[94] This was the text which inspired the Arts and Crafts Movement internationally. It also fed into the Socialist endeavour before the Great War.

So how did Ruskin define the Gothic? 'Pointed arches do not constitute Gothic, nor vaulted roofs, nor flying buttresses, nor grotesque sculptures; but all or some of these things [are there], and many other things with them, when they come together so as to have life.'[95] Life is more important than shape or decoration.

Gothic, he says, is flexible and organic. It works on any scale, and in any type of building, from a farmyard to a cathedral: 'It can shrink into a turret, expand into a hall, coil into a staircase, or spring into a spire, with undegraded grace and unexhausted energy'. Gothic is full of surprises, 'saying new and different things'. An architect, like a novelist, should not rely on repetition, they should not be boring. And great Gothic art is recognised by its refusal to stick to convention. 'If they wanted a window, they opened one; a room, they added one; a buttress, they built one ... So that, in the best times of Gothic, a useless window would rather have been opened in an unexpected place for the sake of surprise, than a useful one forbidden for the sake of symmetry.'[96]

This idea of symmetry particularly angered Ruskin. He loathed the matching columns and capitals, the central oblong windows and the even surfaces of buildings inspired by classical Greece or Rome. He saw no opportunities in the stuccoed crescents of Regency London or Leamington Spa for builders to use their initiative, or show their connection with the natural world. 'Wherever the workman is utterly enslaved,' Ruskin wrote, 'the parts of the building must of course be absolutely like each other; for the perfection of his execution can only be reached by exercising him in doing one thing, and giving him nothing else to do.'[97] He sums up this argument: 'if one part always answers accurately to another part, it is sure to be a bad building'.[98]

Ruskin looks to certain elements of a church or palace, particularly the windows and the uprights. He asks us to think about the columns and how the building sits between the earth and the sky. Does it feel as if the vaults and window frames were 'bones of a limb or fibres of a tree', with 'an elastic tension and communication of force'? And he imagines the development of traceries, as 'penetrations through the stone work of windows or walls, cut into forms which looked like stars when seen from within, and leaves when seen from without'.[99] There is always a connectedness to nature, a recognition of what can be learnt from the strength of trees and the mobility of leaves.

He suggests six characteristics to help identify a true Gothic building. The list is typically idiosyncratic, but it does open up new ways of thinking about structure and decoration. It also focuses on the intentions of the architect and workers, as much as on the finished building. There should be savageness, changefulness, naturalism, grotesqueness, rigidity and redundance. Gothic art is never perfect. It is strange and bold, never spare, never simply pretty, and always rooted in an understanding of nature. 'To the Gothic workman,' Ruskin wrote, 'the living foliage became a subject of intense affection ... the love of change ... is at once soothed and satisfied as it watches the wandering of the tendril and the budding of the flower.'[100]

As with any great love story, the intensity of Ruskin's desire to explore and get under the skin of the city began to wear off. He saw the sad decline in Venice's fortunes, which seemed to be played out in the architecture. He had seen it happen in northern France too, but here the city's infidelity to the Gothic in all its lively forms hit him even harder. He wrote sadly, 'The Gothic fell, because its wealth was empty, and its profusion heartless'. [101]

Ruskin's disenchantment with Venice was gradual. When he visited in the late 1840s, Venice was under Austrian occupation. It had been besieged and bombarded, and was in a dismal state: 'Buckets were set on the floor of the Scuola di San Rocco, in every shower, to catch the rain which came though the pictures of Tintoret on the ceiling'.[102] He came to see the city 'more and more as a vain temptation' and was dismayed by the impact of the Renaissance on Venetian ideas and architecture. He dated the downfall of Italian Gothic very precisely between 1423 and 1480, his dates for the births of Giovanni Bellini and Titian. The midpoint of this decline was the fall of Constantinople to the Turks in 1453.

There was of course a moralistic angle to his criticism. It became a question of sensuality and intemperance. He was dismayed by the 'coarseness in curvature ... lusciousness in arrangement of line' and a rejection of 'the true beauty of chaste form and restrained form' in later buildings. He upbraided his readers that they still could not recognise the 'essential difference between chasteness and extravagance'.[103] He pointed to the carving of leaves on the capitals around the city. At their best, the artists responded to the natural world with great sensitivity and delicacy. 'The Gothic mind,' he said, enjoyed 'the oak, thorn, and thistle', and the 'builder of the Ducal Palace . . . delighted in this breadth as nature delights in the sweeping freshness of the dock-leaf or water-lily.'[104] But it did not last.

He wrote of the city (always female),

in the final period of her decline: a ghost upon the sands of the sea, so weak – so quiet, – so bereft of all but her loveliness, that we might well doubt, as we watched her faint reflection in the mirage of the lagoon, which was the City, and which the Shadow. I would endeavour to trace the lines of this image before it be for ever lost, and to record, as far as I may, the warning which seems to me to be uttered by every one of the fast-gaining waves, that beat like passing bells, against the Stones of Venice.[105]

And yet, with his own writings, and his desire to preserve, to teach and share his love, he brought more visitors to the city. This sense that Venice might slip away, and be lost before it could be seen, has drawn so many travellers that they now clog the canals and obscure the vistas they came to admire.

Chapter 4

Travelling

The Exterior of the Ducal Palace, Venice

Ruskin's Venice was war-torn and empty. It was cold and poor. Still, he was infatuated, and poured out his heart, creating love poems to the buildings he desired to know and save. Ruskin's description of the basilica of St Mark's is tender and sensual. It is the love letter he never wrote to his wife. She sat in her box at the opera besieged by eager young men, while he conceived this glowing paragraph:

there rises a vision out of the earth, and all the great square seems to have opened from it in a kind of awe, that we may see it far away; – a multitude of pillars and white domes, clustered into a long low pyramid of coloured light; a treasure heap – it seems, partly of gold, and partly of opal and mother-of-pearl, hollowed beneath into five great vaulted porches, ceiled with fair mosaic, and beset with sculpture of alabaster, clear as amber and delicate as ivory ... and in the midst of it, the solemn forms of angels, sceptred and robed to the feet, and leaning to each other across the gates . . . – a confusion of delight, amidst which the breasts of the Greek horses are seen blazing in their breadth of golden strength, and the St Mark's lion, lifted on a blue field covered with stars, until at last, as if in ecstasy, the crests of the arches break into a marble foam; and toss themselves far into the blue sky in flashes and wreaths of sculptured spray, as if the breakers on the Lido shore had been frost-bound before they fell, and the sea-nymphs had inlaid them with coral and amethyst.[106]

Ruskin and his beloved city are now woven together through their shared history. They have come to define each other, for better and for worse.

'This is not Veniceland'

There are turnstiles at the Calatrava bridge and outside the Santa Lucia train station. The police will be checking. Do you have the correct documentation? Are you a local? Are you a day tripper? There are plans for segregated access to the city, and a 'one-in, one-out' policy. The inundation of tourists over Easter weekend has put the authorities on the alert. Venice can no longer cope. The trickle of outsiders who visited in Ruskin's day has swollen beyond all imagining. Coach tours, backpackers eating their ice cream on the steps of the palazzi, 'Jewels of the Mediterranean' cruisers, art lovers and bucket-listers, together they are overwhelming the city.

The permanent residents are dwindling, with only 55,000 people now living in Venice. (At the end of the Second World War, there had been 190,000). On one bright spring day, over 60,000 visitors flooded in, causing impossible queues for the water buses and the Piazza San Marco. Venice and the Venetians can't survive with thirty million visitors a year passing across their bridges.

But is it right to stop travellers on the threshold of Venice? Or to tell them to put away their phones and look directly at the beautiful buildings reflected in the lagoon? Is it elitist and unhelpful to ask visitors to come face to face with the paintings? All too often gallery audiences now stand with their backs to the art as they take a selfie to share. Who will benefit from this encounter? Of the eighty exchange students on the coach, seventy-nine might be there for the Instagram shots. What if just one finds this a life-changing day? One young woman, going home to Glasgow or Chicago or Seoul, thinking, 'Now I see. Now I understand. Now I know what to do next.' That surely would be enough.

After the record-breaking crowds in April 2018, it is clear that the current numbers are unsustainable. Gates at the entry points to the city are one solution, but they are not popular with visitors or locals. Business owners and local campaigners agree that it is impossible to live with the '*Bollino Nero*' (Code

Black) conditions. They argue that the turnstiles simply turn the city into a theme park, rather than a living community. 'This is not Veniceland,' they protest. Some say that visitors should have to book in advance, and 'include some financial contribution to maintaining . . . the most beautiful city in the world'. Others worry about crushes and flashpoints when police close the gates. Tommaso Cacciari, who campaigns against the vast cruise ships that dwarf the domes and campanile, says that local government should focus on keeping the city alive with more affordable permanent housing. 'The metal barriers,' he says, 'show that our home is already a museum and entertainment park.'[107]

Has Ruskin created this monster? Can we blame him for our desire to see St Mark's with our own eyes, to photograph the Bridge of Sighs, to swoon beneath a Veronese? Indiscriminate sightseeing was already a problem in his lifetime. And by 1908, less than a decade after Ruskin's death, E.M. Forster could create the awful Eleanor Lavish, in *A Room with a View*, who 'would like to set an examination paper at Dover and turn back every tourist who couldn't pass it.'[108] Are we on her side, limiting access to those who care and look 'properly'? Or should we say, with William Morris, 'I do not want Art for a few, any more than I want Education for a few, or Freedom for a few.'[109] Where would Ruskin stand on democratisation and contact with fragile, lovely things?

Ruskin knew that, unwittingly, he was part of the problem. He was uncomfortable with the developing taste for travel that he witnessed in the mid-century. Like many other leisured families, the Ruskins took advantage of peace in Europe, especially between the end of the 1848 revolutions and the start of the Franco-Prussian war in 1870. These journeys formed the bedrock of his popular writings, including *The Seven Lamps of Architecture* and *The Stones of Venice*. At the same time, rolling out the rail networks gave unprecedented opportunities for middle-class tourism. Ruskin loathed the railways. Still, he recognised that his enthusiastic essays and lectures pointed out places that had previously been overlooked. This is not a new phenomenon, our search for the 'unspoilt'. It is not an invention of the colour supplement: last year, a flower farm on the Isles of Scilly; this year, skiing in Romania; next year, cruising the North-West Passage.

Ruskin dealt with the increased appetite for art and travel in two ways. Firstly, he believed that if people were going to make the journey, they should at least know what they were looking at. So he wrote guidebooks. And, secondly, he said that it was not always possible (or desirable) to see the real thing. He found ways to bring beauty and history back to his audiences in Britain. For those who could not travel, he commissioned copies, created museums, gave lectures, encouraged discussion groups, and showed them what was closer to home. His approach was to educate, to share, and to think around the problem. We do not all need to walk through Venice to appreciate its loveliness. Sometimes we should take a step back.

Mornings in Florence

Ruskin clearly remembered his first sight of San Miniato, the hill town above Florence. This was in 1845, in the days before parties of tourists came to look at the view. He reached the little town 'through small rural vineyards'. The church 'stood deserted, but not ruinous, with a narrow lawn of scented herbage before it, and sweet wild weeds about its steps, all shut in by a hedge of roses.'

Mostly, that summer, he spent his time in Santa Maria Novella, studying paintings of 'angel or prophet, knight or hermit, girl or goddess, prince or peasant'. He came to love the frescoes in 'the Ghirlandajo apse. There were no services behind the high altar; tourists, even the most learned, had never in those days heard Ghirlandajo's name'. He worked 'seated mostly astride on the [choir's] desks, till I tumbled off backwards one day at the gap where the steps went down.' He was too busy looking up and sketching. In the sacristy, he drew Fra Angelico's *Annunciation*: 'the monks let me sit close to it and work, as long as I liked, and went on with their cup-rinsings and cope-foldings without minding me'.[110] No one else seemed much interested in the art of the fifteenth century. A few artists, a few pioneering collectors were developing a taste for 'Early Italian' altarpieces. In general, visitors to Florence came to admire the old masters, and a tour of the Uffizi would focus on big brown paintings, rather than small blue and gold ones.

By the mid-1870s, when Ruskin wrote his guidebook, *Mornings in Florence*, the city had changed dramatically. The railway station at the east end of Santa Maria Novella opened in 1848, connecting Florence to Pisa. (A two-mile rail bridge connecting Venice to the mainland at Mestre was opened a few years earlier in January 1846.) He had already created a market for thought-provoking art criticism in *Modern Painters* and *The Stones of Venice*. Now his readers were setting their sights on Tuscany, and wanted to know where to look.

Ruskin is an exacting companion. He expects us to have some grasp of history, ancient and early modern, and a degree of self-control: 'My general directions to all young people going to Florence or Rome would be very short: "Know your first volume of Vasari, and your first two books of Livy; look about you, and don't talk, nor listen to talking."'[111] Maybe some Interrailers will still be carrying Vasari in their rucksacks. (I know I did, dog-eared, Sellotaped and full of underlinings, tucked in my bag beside a photocopy of 'The Nature of Gothic', ready for when we reached Venice). Fewer will now be familiar with Livy's *History of Rome*. But using our eyes is the harder task. Picking our way through the intricacies of late medieval iconography is tough.

Ruskin also recognises that most of his readers lack his stamina. He begins his close examination of one of the wall paintings in the Spanish Chapel, a complex sequence of fourteenth-century frescoes, with a question: 'How long do you think it will take you, or ought to take, to see such a picture?' And then he seems to laugh. Often Ruskin sounds so serious. But he can be amusing and affectionate, catching us off guard with an unexpected turn of phrase. He acknowledges that we are pressed for time: 'You have probably allowed half-an-hour for Santa Maria Novella; half-an-hour for San Lorenzo; an hour for the museum of sculpture at the Bargello; an hour for shopping; and then it will be lunch time, and you mustn't be late, because you are to leave by the afternoon train, and must positively be in Rome tomorrow morning.' He calculates how much of the half-hour in Santa Maria Novella can be allotted to the Spanish Chapel: 'at the utmost, a quarter of an hour . . . That will give you two minutes and a half for each side, two for the ceiling', and three minutes reading the guidebook. 'Two minutes and a half you have got, then – (and I observed during my five weeks' work in the chapel that English visitors seldom gave so much) – to read this scheme given you by Simon Memmi of human spiritual education.'[112] We seem to be a lost cause. But still he presses on. He has spent his five weeks up scaffolding, making notes on colours and costumes, on medieval saints and virtues, so that we don't have to. He has decoded the symbolism, the crystal balls and musical instruments held by the rows of holy figures. On the far wall, he points out to us the portraits of the poet Petrarch and his beloved Laura, 'with a little tongue of fire between her breast and throat'.[113]

Is all this work for our sake or for his? He still feels that he has barely scratched the surface, barely understood a quarter of one of the great wall paintings in this chapel. He asks us to come back with him, if we have time, tomorrow morning. But, like Lucy Honeychurch in *A Room with a View*, most of his readers hardly get to see what they thought they were looking for – in her case, a view of the Arno. They are 'handed about like a parcel of goods from Venice to Florence, Florence to Rome, living herded together in pensions or hotels ... their one anxiety to get "done" or "through" and go on somewhere else'.[114] Looking well is complicated and time-consuming. Florence seems full of things we don't want to miss. And we have to be moving on.

Still, we can take Ruskin with us, in our pockets, on our Kindles. We are fortunate in this digitised age. We no longer have to find our way to a university library, hoping that they will have hung on to the thirty-nine volumes of his *Collected Works*, to discover what he has to say about our favourite cathedral, or an Alpine view. We can sit on the train or in the airport, following his texts.

Carefully Ruskin shares the knowledge he has gathered over many months. His approach is unconventional, and often partial. But he has recognised the time and effort the artists put in to create the Spanish Chapel. He believes they deserve our time and concentration too. With his help we can find our way through the complexities, until they begin to make some sense. Patterns emerge, and a different world view seems to turn towards us. What mattered to these artists? How did they imagine heaven or beauty or good government? Ruskin unravels these stories. He shows the female figures who represent the ideal education: Grammar, Rhetoric, Logic, Music and so on. He explains how they are paired with Old Testament figures, and how the objects they hold – scrolls, scorpions, budding twigs – underline their qualities. Ruskin questions which parts are original, and which are repainted. And above all, he encourages us to think about what is worth looking at. In all the grand muddle of the figures heaped upon figures, all the allegories and Bible tales, the damned and the saved, and those waiting in limbo, he points out one face or gesture, and encourages us to savour it.

His description of the figure of Music in the Spanish Chapel is something that we can enjoy even if we can no longer stand beneath 'the vaulted book'. Look, he says. 'After learning to reason, you will learn to sing; for you will want to. There is so much reason for singing in the sweet world, when one thinks rightly of it.'[115] He singles out Music because she is 'one of the loveliest in the series', full of 'extreme refinement and tender severity . . . the face thin, abstracted, wistful; the lips not far open in their low singing; . . . the actions of both hands are singularly sweet.' Ruskin has stopped not just to look, but to listen to this young woman, to watch her lips and her fingers as she plays a tiny Gothic organ. 'She is keeping down one note only, with her third finger, seen under the raised fourth: the thumb, just passing under' as she is about to move to the next note in her tune.[116] This is enough for us to contemplate: a singing girl, undamaged by restoration, crowned with leaves, and her hair rippling to her shoulders. Ruskin has shown us this, and thankfully we can bring her with us. We cannot comprehend the full sweep of the artists' plans for spiritual and secular education. Instead we can remember her, and next time we are in Florence, perhaps we will make a point of visiting the chapel to take another look.

Afternoons in Sheffield

But what if we cannot afford to visit Florence? What should we do if we're worried about Venice sinking beneath the tide of tourists? Ruskin also had the answer for this. As well as painting prose pictures for us of the most delightful things to see, he made copies to bring home. He recognised the importance of universal education, and what we now call lifelong learning. He was particularly concerned with communities of craftspeople whom he believed would benefit from seeing new and wonderful things. So he made a gift to the people of Sheffield, to encourage all comers to find refreshment in art and nature. The collections of the Ruskin museum include hundreds of drawings, watercolours and plaster casts of places that mattered to Ruskin, alongside prints, rocks, books, and suggestions about how we might enjoy them.

Ruskin had always collected images of the places he visited.

Much of his own early impetus to travel had sprung from pictures he had seen – in Turner's illustrations of *Italy* (poems by Samuel Rogers) and the portfolio of prints of *Flanders and Germany* by Prout. As a result, he understood the potential for imaginative journeys. He developed a system of drawing as he travelled, 'of making scrawls as the carriage went along, and working them up' when they reached the hotel.[117] Often, however, these were not enough, so with his valet, George Crawley, he began to make daguerreotype photographs of buildings and sights that he knew were under threat. They were probably the first people to photograph the massive Mer de Glace near Chamonix. Ruskin was fascinated by geology as well as the potential for this new technology, and he wanted to understand how the landscape was shifting year by year.

Over time, these personal memoranda evolved into something more public. The photographs and diagrams were reprinted as illustrations to his books. His watercolours and plaster casts were used to demonstrate the destruction of significant buildings, sometimes through demolition, sometimes through unsympathetic restoration. Ruskin commissioned casts to be made of the capitals of the Ducal Palace in Venice, for example, or carvings on French churches. Now they are often the only remnant of a beloved building, recorded before they succumbed to acid rain, or an overzealous architect. The technique of casting directly from the stone had been used by museums and art schools from the mid-nineteenth century to create teaching aids and spectacular exhibits, like the Cast

Courts at South Kensington (now the V&A Museum). It was non-invasive and extremely accurate.

Ruskin transformed this ability to make detailed copies into a political tool. In particular, during his campaign against the stripping of the facade of St Mark's, Venice, this was one of his strategies – to make copies and share them, in water-colour and plaster cast. In his open letter demanding an end to the restoration, he explained that there was little else he could do, except show his own carefully coloured drawings and a series of photographs to raise awareness of what was being lost. He also issued a call to arms for 'friends . . . and my fellow-workers, to get such casts, and colourings, and measurings, as may be of use in time to come.' He ends with an idiosyncratic flourish, mourning these copies, as 'Frag-mentary enough they must be – poor fallen plumes of the winged lion's wings'.[118] He paid £500 for a massive painting of the whole of the western facade, created by John Bunney, as part of his philanthropic venture, the Guild of St George. He explained that he could have more casts made, but 'can no more pay for them out of my own pocket'.[119]

By his influence and his agitation, Ruskin was successful in stopping the disastrous work on St Mark's. His work also benefited those who would never see Venice in person. Many of the copies he commissioned were given to his museum in Walkley, three miles outside the centre of Sheffield. The site was deliberately chosen. It was to be a destination, the end point of a pleasant stroll up from the city. The walk and the objects on display were equal parts of the project. Visitors could enjoy the exercise and the view of the Rivelin and Loxley valleys before stepping inside, to explore further afield. (Since the collections have moved to the Millennium Galleries in the heart of Sheffield, visitors now hear recordings of birdsong as they enter the modern space, to remind us of the origins of Ruskin's enterprise.)

The gallery was free to visit, and still is. It was open every day except Thursdays, from nine a.m. to nine p.m. This allowed working people to make their pilgrimage after work. And it was filled with marvels, collected by Ruskin on his journeys. Studies of stained glass from Santa Croce were shown alongside Kate Greenaway's drawings of moss and ivy. Turner engravings hung next to architectural watercolours of Verona and Bergamo. The display was dense and multi-layered, encouraging visitors to think across time and place. Mineral samples, sculpture, photographs all offered different ways into the collections.

One wall focused on Venice. Bunney's magnificent oil painting of St Mark's was the centrepiece, surrounded by plaster casts from the basilica and the Doge's Palace. Then there were five bright blue-and-gold studies of the mosaics from inside the domes of St Mark's. Ruskin had chosen elements of this building, 'the most rich in associations, the most marvellous in beauty, the most perfect in preservation'.[120] He had brought these wonders to Sheffield, to sit near casts from Rouen cathedral. Here were his own drawings of Pisa, there a watercolour of Giotto's tower in Florence. In a display case was a collection of medieval manuscripts; a fifteenth-century French book of hours and a twelfth-century German lectionary. The Gothic world could be discovered in an afternoon. There were even a couple of chairs for visitors to sit down and look more comfortably.

How were the working people of Sheffield supposed to respond to the fragmentary glories of Italy? Ruskin suggested that the best museum should 'give little, but that little good and beautiful'. And, he said, 'explain it thoroughly'. It was no good lining up 'a thousand specimens ... what is the use of that to a man who has only a quarter of an hour to spare in a week?'[121]

However Ruskin expected visitors to put in some effort, to meet the artists halfway. His response to a Sheffield man who complained that 'he couldn't see anything' in a work of art was direct. He did not set up the museum for amusement but for education. 'The Lippi, and the Titian, and the Velasquez are ... alike in one quality ... They are work of men doing their best. And whose pride is in doing their best and most.'[122] He emphasised the striving, the training, the order and obedience shown by the artists he chose to exhibit.

At its heart, this enterprise was not simply about collecting lovely things to entertain Yorkshiremen and women. The museum was part of Ruskin's attempt to transform ideas about government and economics in the city, through fellowship and cooperation. Yes, visitors came to Walkley to look at the pictures. They also came to talk and to ask questions. The museum was a meeting place. Ruskin hoped that those who came would be encouraged to turn their hands and minds to new things. He wanted the metalworkers of Sheffield to think differently about their own skills, and to take pride in their productions.

Even now, although the collections have moved, in Walkley there are still projects that have grown out of Ruskin's venture. Community workers are bringing people together to make and question, to share their knowledge of history or of nature, in Ruskin's name. And the Ruskin Collection in the city centre of Sheffield opens its doors every day to everyone: shoppers, parents with pushchairs, eager students and people with nowhere in particular to be. For some, Italy is still too far off.

Ruskin recognised this. So he did what he could to make his choice of French, German, Italian and Spanish art accessible to those who never travelled beyond the seven hills of Sheffield. He knew that he could not expect all his readers to follow him to Venice. But for those who did, he told them to 'go first into the Piazetta, and stand anywhere in the shade, where you can well see its two granite pillars'.[123] From there he could unfold the tales of Tyre and Byzantium, and the birth of the great floating city. Ruskin's guidebook to Venice, *St Mark's Rest*, was the culmination of long months, indeed years of looking, that had begun with *The Stones of Venice*.

On foot

Ruskin had leisure for slow travel. He was not compelled to squeeze all his journeys into two-week's annual leave, or a half-term holiday. He could take his time, walking or gliding through Venice in a gondola. He had grown accustomed to this pace of movement as a child, when he and his parents had travelled to Italy and back 'with post-horses, and, on the lakes, with oared boats'. They 'went from forty to fifty miles a day, starting always early enough in the morning to arrive comfortably to four o'clock dinner. Generally, therefore, getting off at six o'clock, a stage or two were done before breakfast, with the dew on the grass, and first scent from the hawthorns'.[124] Travelling itself was a pleasure, by carriage or boat, or especially on foot.

Ruskin loved walking. He enjoyed feeling connected to the earth. He could take in the landscape more slowly and stop to examine plants or rocks in more detail. Many of his most vivid passages of writing begin with the sensation of moving quietly across country, the view opening out before us. He incorporates touch and sound and scent as he walks through a meadow and into a wood in Switzerland:

Such grass, for strength, and height and loveliness, I never saw – all blue too with masses of salvia, and flamed with gold, yet quiet and solemn in its own green depth; the air was full of the scent of the living grass and new-mown hay, the sweet breathing of the honeysuckle and narcissus shed up on it at intervals, mixed with the sound of streams, and the clear thrill of birds' voices far away . . . – that indescribable turf, soft like some rich, smooth fur, running in bays and inlets and bright straits and shadowy creeks and gulphs in among the forest, calm, upright, unentangled forest . . . no wildness, nor crowding; no withering.[125]

This direct experience is lost when we watch the world through a windscreen. Ruskin reminds us of the value of walking. When he moved to the Lake District he walked constantly. Six or seven miles, to the Old Man of Coniston and back, seemed nothing to him.

Despite his public image as a scholar, Ruskin was never desk-bound. Even when he was ill, he would set out from his home at Brantwood, into his garden, down to the lakeside or up into the hills, trying to settle his thoughts. 'I look at the water a while, can't make it out,' he wrote in his diary. 'Went then into my field – to and fro there, thinking of my Father. Down into the road. Saw light of moonrise. Walked to end of lower field – & then back to Lodge.'[126] He often thought of his father as he measured the land with his stride. His father's money had paid for Brantwood. His father's work had given Ruskin the taste for travel.

Ruskin's father, John James, did have to work for his living, as a sherry importer. But most years he managed to combine visiting his customers with a tour of the more picturesque parts of England, and sometimes Wales and Scotland. These journeys were never rushed. 'We were never in a hurry,' Ruskin recalled, 'always starting at the hour we chose, and that if we weren't ready, the horses would wait.'[127] As a young boy, he would perch on his seat at the front of the carriage and watch the country unfold. As he grew older, he would jump down and walk alongside his parents, gathering specimens and making swift sketches.

He never learnt to ride with confidence. Ruskin was sad about this. He wished his parents had given him 'a shaggy scrap of a Welsh pony, and left me in charge of a good Welsh guide'. Instead, he was taken by his father every week to a 'sawdust-floored prison of a riding-school in Moorfields, the smell of which, as we turned in at the gate of it, was a terror and horror and abomination to me: and there I was put on big horses that jumped, and reared, and circled, and sidled; and fell off them regularly'.[128] He gave up.

From the ground he noticed things that other people overlooked. The colour of the earth, the sound it made as he walked over it, the plants that sprang up, the water that flowed. One of his most unexpected and moving lectures began on a visit to Tunbridge Wells. 'In my walk', he saw 'the welling forth of the spring over the orange rim of its marble basin. The memory of the clear water, sparkling over its saffron stain, came back to me as the strongest image connected with the place.' The iron in the Wells 'stains the great earth', and Ruskin took it for the subject of his speech.[129] He began to imagine the landscape without iron, 'dirty white – the white of thaw, with all the chill of snow in it, but none of its brightness. That is what the colour of the earth would be without its iron.' The ploughed fields of Kent, 'like deep folds of a mantle of russet velvet – fancy it all changed suddenly into grisly furrows in a field of mud'. That would be the world without iron, which is 'the sunshine and light of landscape'.[130] Ruskin spent a lifetime looking up and looking down, thinking of how things are connected – geology, chemistry, associations of warmth and cold, the weight of soil on our boots, the imprint we make with each step.

Ruskin started 'The Work of Iron' with the remembrance of falling water, and ended with a sermon on the use and misuse of natural resources in mines or factories. He questioned how we fence our neighbours out or in with iron railings. He asked about how we make war, and what we waste in conflict. All this effort, he suggested, was misplaced. If only we could better understand the wealth and generosity of the earth, the digging, the ploughing, the springs of water. So often, we mar what we come to admire. We find something rich or beautiful in the landscape, and we spoil it.

There was a quiet corner of Herne Hill in south London that Ruskin often called to mind. It was near where he grew up. He used to walk 'through a mile of chestnut, lilac, and apple trees' to a 'great field' filled with cows and buttercups.

Since the Crystal Palace was moved there – a monstrous misuse of iron and glass in Ruskin's eyes – the quiet loveliness was lost. Instead, 'a flood of pedestrians . . . left it filthy with cigar ashes.' And then came the 'excursion train', filled with unthinking visitors 'who knocked the palings about, roared at the cows, and tore down what branches of blossom they could reach'.[131] This was what he called 'the modern steam-puffed tourist.' He would have agreed with the sentiments of today's environmentalists and 'slow travellers', who have paraphrased the words of Chief Seattle/Si'ahl, 'Take nothing but photographs; leave nothing but footprints; keep nothing but memories.'

If Ruskin loved walking, he hated the railways. He fought against the expansion of the network into the Lake District. He avoided travelling by train as far as he could. He was fortunate. He and his parents could afford to hire private carriages, all carefully kitted out, when they went on their expeditions. He knew that these family journeys seemed tame, to the 'young people nowadays, or even lively old ones', who 'travel more in search of adventures than of information . . . Yet the meek ignorance has these advantages. We did not travel for adventures, nor for company, but to see with our eyes, and to measure with our hearts.'[132]

So why do we travel now? Are we looking for thrills, or to tick Venice off the list? Do we pay attention to the detritus we leave in our wake, or the people who service our needs? In our hurry, we seem so often to miss the point. The climbing

111

gear littering the slopes of Everest; the cruise ships cluttering up the harbours of Lerwick or Dubrovnik; the rapidly retreating Mer de Glace, melting forty metres a year, and Ruskin's favourite walking trails collapsing – these are all side-effects of global tourism.[133] Every plane journey, every road trip, comes at a cost. We have made this mess. But it is not news. Ruskin has been spelling it out to us for 150 years.

The cities Ruskin loved, already damaged by ill-conceived restoration, were being engulfed by pollution even in his day. As he wrote to his friend Lady Simon: 'Our Geneva – Our Como – Our Verona – *twice* dead – and plucked up by the roots'.[134]

And, beyond the surface of the buildings, Ruskin recognised that something else was being tarnished: the lives of the people who moved through them. As early as 1865, he tried to show that our environment and our well-being are entangled:

All lovely architecture was designed for cities in cloudless air; for . . . cities built that men might live happily in them, and take delight daily in each other's presence and powers. But our cities, built in black air which, by its accumulated foulness, first renders all ornament invisible in distance, and then chokes its interstices with soot . . . cities in which the object of men is not life, but labour; and in which the streets are not the avenues for the passing and procession of a happy people, but the drains for the discharge of a tormented mob, in which the only object in reaching any spot is to be transferred to another; in which existence becomes mere transition, and every creature is only one atom in a drift of human dust, and current of interchanging particles, circulating here by tunnels underground, and there by tubes in the air; for a city, or cities, such as this no architecture is possible – nay, no desire of it is possible to their inhabitants.[135]

Ruskin feared for the future of the modern industrial city, as much as for the medieval cities which he was trying to preserve. He was looking forward as well as back. He wanted people to be able to move freely, but thoughtfully. To use his memorable phrase, when we travel, we should be more than 'one atom in a drift of human dust'. Travel should be joyful. Moving over the earth, taking pleasure in our direct experience, wholeheartedly.

I am not planning to return to Venice, for all its lovely architecture. My heart is not in it. I don't expect to revisit Giotto's little painted chapel in Padua either, with its timed ticketing and airlocks. I'm in no rush to see Botticelli's *Primavera* again in Florence. Our breath, the warmth of our bodies, our constant footfall will be taking its toll on the fragile layers of 500-year-old paint. Instead I will remember the bright mornings when I first saw these things. I have my clear recollections, I have photographs and books. I have

Ruskin's words to show me what I am missing. And if I really want to understand the best of their beauty, and the way they looked before the crowds came, I will go to Sheffield instead. There perhaps, walking quietly among Ruskin's own collection, we can see with our eyes and measure with our hearts.

Chapter 5

Loving

Rose La Touche

Jessie. Adèle. Charlotte. Effie. Rose.

These were the girls that Ruskin loved and lost. And cousin Joanie – she stayed close, living with him to the end. But Joanie married Arthur. There has been so much speculation over the years about Ruskin's impotency, his sexuality. It has clouded his reputation; he is laughed at as a prude and the worst kind of uptight misogynist. His marriage was a failure. Ruskin admitted later that he was 'disgusted' by the body of his teenage wife, Effie. They never had sex on their honeymoon, nor in the six years they were married after that. Effie left him for Millais, his younger, more successful protégé. Ruskin watched her go without a fight and went off on holiday in Switzerland with his parents. His father said that they were all glad to be clear of his 'commonplace Scotch wife'.

Recently, there is the inevitable question at every lecture I give: 'Was Ruskin a paedophile?' How can we explain his obsessive devotion to Rose La Touche? He was her teacher, yet he wanted to marry her as soon as she turned eighteen. His friends advised him to tone down his references to Rose in his public writings, but Ruskin felt he had nothing to hide. Should we try to understand his affections, sympathise with him? Where should we place his relationships with his pupils on the sliding scale from unprofessional to abusive? Can we learn anything from Ruskin about loving, or loving well? Can we begin to understand the sadness of getting it wrong? His behaviour was dubious then, as it seems creepy now – even if we bear in mind that the age of consent was only raised to sixteen in the 1880s. But we should also remember that Ruskin's response to his beloved girls was invariably 'look but don't touch'. It was their innocence he loved, their fresh and unself-conscious beauty, their flattery.

Ruskin's aversion to mature women and grown-up relationships is unsettling. To modern eyes it seems more predatory than peculiar. His insistence on writing to his cousin Joanie in a childish, lisping, private language well into his sixties is very odd indeed. Ruskin never settled to a job, never had to fit into adult systems of work or family. His clear-sighted comments often come from a place of detachment. He was always the spoilt only child, long after his parents had died.

Mama and Papa

It may sound overdetermined, but Ruskin's problems with love stemmed from his protective parents. Ruskin was excited by the sensuality of the eye. Other forms of sensuality upset him. They were associated with sinfulness. In *Modern Painters* he writes extensively about his love of looking at beautiful things, but was aware that even this could be a slippery slope, when perceptions of the beautiful became 'a mere minister to their desires, and accompaniment and seasoning of lower sensual pleasures, until all their emotions take the same earthly stamp, and the sense of beauty sinks into the servant of lust'.[136]

Lust. Earthly emotions. Desires. Lower pleasures. His mother had schooled him well in her Evangelical Protestant principles. She saw temptation in every weakness, and decadence in anything smacking of delight. Of course, Ruskin's account of his own childhood in *Praeterita* is partial. He wanted to justify his lifestyle and actions. So we must read it as one-sided. But the vivid imagery he places on the page does tally with the experiences of friends who met him and his parents in later life. The child who was always whipped when he cried. The mother who 'forced me, by steady daily toil, to learn long chapters of the Bible by heart; as well as to read it every syllable through, aloud, hard names and all, from Genesis to the Apocalypse, about once a year'.[137] Forcing, not encouraging. Narrowing, not enlightening. His parents fretted and scolded him about his health, physical and religious, but could not help him to understand his young bride.

What did Ruskin learn about love at home? When he writes about his boyhood, there is always a feeling of restraint.

His parents showed him little physical or emotional warmth. Although they are the most dominant characters in his autobiography, Ruskin's abiding memory of his home, was 'that I had nothing to love'. Yes, he enjoyed peace, and faith, and 'obeyed word, or lifted finger, of father or mother, simply as a ship her helm'. But no love. 'My parents were,' he wrote, 'visible powers of nature to me, no more loved than the sun and the moon.' He was completely safe, completely supported, but he had no independence, no test of his patience, never experienced 'trouble or disorder ... or anxiety'. Looking back, he realised what he had missed. 'The bridle and blinkers were never taken off me. Children should have their times of being off duty, like soldiers.'[138]

Ruskin's experience of sweetness was so limited that he remembered his first taste of custard – when he had the scrapings from the bottom of his father's dish – and 'I recollect,' he wrote, 'my mother giving me three raisins, in the forenoon, out of the store cabinet.'[139] He was physically so cosseted that an excursion to the hills near Tintern and Malvern became a cherished memory, because he 'was allowed to run free on them, there being no precipices to fall over nor streams to fall into.'[140] When his mother was around, he could not go to the edge of a pond, or be in the same field as a pony.

Running free, tasting sweetness, embracing, Ruskin was hungry for these joys. But he was scared of them too. He felt his mother watching him, and his father judging every action. Even writing his memoirs, he felt their weight. Ruskin began, as he said, his 'prefatory words on my father's birthday, in what was once my nursery in his old house'. He had been four when his parents had brought him up to this room. That was sixty-two years before. For Ruskin, the story of his own life was, above all, 'a dutiful offering at the grave' of his parents.[141]

He knew a little about his own parents' courtship and marriage but it was tainted with suicide and secrecy. Ruskin's paternal grandfather tried to kill himself with his cut-throat razor. Ruskin's mother Margaret found him in his bedroom, covered in blood, and did her best to patch him up. The doctor could not save him, and the trauma of this bloody event never left her. She felt unlucky, and loathed the house where it happened – Bowerswell near Perth. (It was bought by the Gray family when John James and Margaret moved to London.)

Ruskin's account of his parents' long engagement and quiet wedding makes it sound more like a business trans-action than a romance. Margaret Cox was four years older than her cousin John James, and had been rescued from the ignominy of growing up in a pub. She acted as housekeeper to her wealthier relatives, and John James thought of her as a 'mildly liked – governess and confidante . . . in all his flashingly transient amours'. Eventually, as Ruskin put it, 'my father chose his wife much with the same kind of serenity and decision with which afterwards he chose his clerks.' She was not 'an ideal heroine', but rather 'the best sort of person he could have for a wife'.[142] Where was the spark, the longing?

Mild liking seems too feeble a foundation for a lifelong relationship. But it was evidently enough for Margaret, who waited until she was pushing forty to be married.

Margaret proudly told her son this tale of limited enthusiasm and secrecy, and Ruskin accepted his parents' disdain for passion for many years. But the constant, inhibiting sense of duty and self-control that they imposed left him vulnerable. His memory of his first friendship with his little cousin Jessie revolves around his desire to rebel, even in a very small way. She was 'traversing a bright space between her sixth and ninth year; dark-eyed deeply' when young Ruskin stayed with her family near Perth on the banks of the Tay. They were told off together for wanting more cream on their porridge, and for jumping off a wooden trunk – and on a Sunday too. '"Never mind, John," said Jessie to me . . . "when we're married, we'll jump off boxes all day long, if we like!"'[143] His mother was somewhere in the background, but on these holidays, the boy was briefly free to dream and play.

'Rippling ecstasies of derision'

His anxiety about physical affection started early. Ruskin fell in love – deeply, painfully, unsuitably – time and again. But he was thwarted by his own upbringing, by the interference of his parents, by the strangeness of their own marriage.

He grew up in the company of young women, and though he was certainly awkward, he was never as isolated as he suggests in his autobiography. Throughout his childhood, he spent holidays with his girl cousins. And when he was ten, Ruskin's mother invited her niece Mary Richardson to live with them, to travel with the family, and study alongside John. He remembered her as 'a rather pretty, blue-eyed, clumsily-made girl', four years older than him. They sat side by side in drawing lessons and sermons, and shared carriage rides around the Lakes, and across the Channel. But he was never in love with Mary. She was, he said, merely a 'serene additional neutral tint in the household harmony'.[144] She never excited any particular affection.

His later loves hit him harder. As Ruskin tried to explain, 'when affection did come, it came with violence utterly rampant and unmanageable.'[145] Ruskin was seventeen. It was summer. His father's Spanish business partner Domecq was visiting British customers, and his four daughters – Adèle Clotilde, Cécile, Elise and Caroline – were welcomed at Herne Hill. They stayed only a few days, but the impact on Ruskin lasted a lifetime. His parents effectively flung him into a bear pit of sophisticated teenage girls and left him to fend for himself. It did not occur to his mother that Ruskin would fall for any of them, as they were all Roman Catholic, and therefore utterly forbidden as objects of desire. Ruskin was smitten, but impossibly awkward in front of these 'Spanish-born, Paris-bred and Catholic-hearted' girls. We can imagine the embarrassment on their side too, as Ruskin sat open-mouthed, looking, he said, like 'a skate in an aquarium trying to get up the glass'. He tried to woo Adèle by harangu-ing her about the Spanish Armada and Catholic doctrines. Then he wrote her a story, in which he played a Neapolitan bandit, and she was 'the Maiden Giuletta'. Unsurprisingly she 'laughed over it in rippling ecstasies of derision'.[146]

Looking back, Ruskin remembered fifteen-year-old Adèle as 'extremely lovely . . . firm, and fiery, and high-principled'. Her father 'was perfectly ready to give me any of his daugh-ters I liked, who could also be got to like me', but thought they should wait a few years. John James Ruskin would have been willing to discuss an engagement. After all, it made good business sense. But Margaret Ruskin was horrified. Her son could not possibly marry a Roman Catholic. It was mon-strous, preposterous, impossible of course. She expected the girls to go back to Paris, and 'Adèle's influence and memory would pass away – with next winter's snow'. Ruskin's response was to sulk and indulge his emotional turmoil by writing a Venetian play about a fair heroine, Bianca. He was 'in a state of majestic imbecility':

I remember nothing more of that year, 1836, than sitting under the mulberry tree in the back garden, writing my tragedy. I forget whether we went travelling or not, or what I did in the rest of the day. It is all now blank to me, except Venice, Bianca, and looking out over Shooter's Hill, where I could see the last turn of the road to Paris.[147]

124

Ruskin had enough self-awareness, finally when he reached his sixties, to recognise what a ridiculous figure he cut. But at the time he was distraught. His misery and the intransigence of his mother made him physically ill. He began coughing blood – a sign of lung disease – and this threw his parents into a fervour of fear. They never forgot this warning – the bloody handkerchief at Ruskin's lips. But it made them even more cosseting and careful.

It took Ruskin several years to recover from his heart-break. By the time he saw Adèle again, she was eighteen and more mature. In Ruskin's eyes she had outgrown her loveli-ness. He felt that his love was 'much too high and fantastic to be diminished by her loss of beauty; but I perfectly well saw and admitted it'.[148] In this first passion we find the pattern that repeated throughout his life. He fell in love with young teenage girls, and lost heart when they grew into women. It is a disturbing emotional weakness, this inability to see beauty in maturity.

At one level, for Ruskin it was a purely aesthetic reaction. Teenage girls are beautiful and full of life and potential. It was not unusual for Victorian artists to try to capture this fragility. It seems disquieting to us now, but his friend Edward Burne-Jones wrote playful and sometimes tender letters to the daughters of his patrons, and painted his own child Margaret as the 'Sleeping Beauty' – always waiting, never kissed. Lewis Carroll's photographs of young Alice are more troubling, but perhaps sit alongside similar 'fancy pictures' made by Julia Margaret Cameron. And Charles Dickens was forty-five when he left his wife for a teenage actress, Nelly Ternan. Although Ruskin's friends recognised that his intense affection for girls like Rose La Touche would harm his reputation, it was more because she was one of the triggers for his mental instability and they wanted to heal that hurt. Finding Rose attractive, and rejoicing in her conversation and company was only part of the problem.

It is very sad now that, as a society, we find it hard to celebrate the loveliness of girls without fear. I know that I am privileged: as the mother of two growing daughters, I can delight in their looks and laughter unreservedly. But I see friends, family and strangers trying to find ways to praise them, worrying about overstepping the mark and saying something inappropriate, shying away from touching. Girlhood is enchanting. Ruskin saw that, but he fell in love with the temporary charms, and struggled to move on. It made him an impossible lover, because no woman can remain seventeen forever. Even Adèle was beautiful only in his memory.

In his mid-twenties, Ruskin showed a brief flurry of interest in a well-connected Scotswoman, Charlotte Lockhart. There is an early picture of her by the pioneering photographers Hill and Adamson taken around the time that Ruskin met her. She was in her late teens, nine years younger than him. Charlotte leans one elbow on a table, and cups her chin to hold her head steady in profile. This will be a long and successful exposure. It is hard to see her expression but she seems to be trying not to laugh. Her dark hair is severely parted across the top of her head, from ear to ear, with a loop of long fringe framing her face, and sweeping round to tuck in at the nape of her neck. She wears a tartan scarf at her neck. It was her Scottishness, and particularly the fact that she was Sir Walter Scott's grand-daughter that attracted Ruskin's attentions. Charlotte became his 'little harebell',[149] mostly because Ruskin was excited at the idea of marrying into the family of his hero. He and his father had a shared love of Scott's novels – they were read aloud in the evenings at home, and were an essential part of Ruskin's upbringing. He and Charlotte met a couple of times at dinner parties, and he decided the best way to impress her was to write her a scholarly article; even Ruskin's father agreed that he was more interesting on paper than in person. Charlotte seems to have been oblivious to his overtures, and a few months later, Ruskin heard that she was engaged elsewhere.

We only know about his interest in Charlotte because Ruskin's mother mentioned her to nineteen-year-old Effie Gray. Euphemia (known as Phemy at home, and called Effie by the Ruskins) was a family friend visiting from Perth in the summer of 1847. Margaret Ruskin was hopeful that her son might make an impression on literary society by a liaison with Scott's grand-daughter. So she warned Effie off. Effie had made quite a name for herself as a young woman 'very forward for her age'. This was not a compliment. And according to the gossips she had received twenty-seven offers of marriage already. Effie was almost certainly engaged to a junior officer when she came south, and from what she knew of romance and flirtation, she could see that Ruskin was not really in love with Miss Lockhart. She told her mother so in one of her letters home.

When Effie came to stay in 1847, it was not her intention to charm him. But within a few months, circumstances had changed in Perth and at Ruskin's home in Denmark Hill. Effie's father had invested unwisely in French railways, and had lost money. There was talk of bankruptcy. He had no settlement to offer any of Effie's potential suitors. She would need to marry someone who was already independently wealthy.

In the meantime, Ruskin's parents had hoped he would 'marry rather high'. His mother, in particular, talked about finding a 'very elegant and high-bred' wife for him. But her young niece, Mary Richardson, had recently married, and left a gap in the household. Who would keep Margaret Ruskin company? Who would travel with the family on their Continental tours, or play the piano in the evening? Effie, who was such an old friend, and so used to the Ruskins and their ways, became more attractive. It would be like gaining a daughter, rather than losing a son. And as his mother reminded him, Ruskin would soon be thirty, and should seriously think about marrying.

Ruskin's engagement was mishandled. He did not speak out openly to Effie when she was with him in London, but waited until she had returned home to Perth. He proposed to her by letter – most of their correspondence around this time no longer exists – and she accepted. She had enjoyed his company, his erudition, the excitement of the art world, and she had few options. Effie could not afford to marry her officer, and there was only one career open to a young woman of her background – she would be a wife, and in due course, a mother. Ruskin threw his heart and soul into his love letters. He had been waiting a very long time to write to a real beloved. Yet Effie still got lectures and sermons among the *tendresses*. She should learn German; her trousseau should be simple and suitable for mountain climbing, rather than grand entrances; she should go to bed early; above all she should be more concerned about her fiancé's needs than the coughs and colds of her little sisters.

Even after more than 150 years, the failure of Effie and Ruskin's honeymoon bothers historians. Ruskin scholars, who are generally very generous-spirited, become anxious and antagonistic over this part of his life. Was Ruskin really impotent? Was Effie an extravagant flirt who took the Ruskins' money and never tried to understand her husband?

It is almost certain that Effie's hairiness was not the sticking point. The date of the wedding changed several times – to suit Ruskin's mother, who did not want the pair to be married in Lent, and Ruskin's father, who wanted them to be home from their honeymoon in time for his birthday. So the difficulty seems to have been that it was the wrong time of the month for Effie. Her bleeding would have embarrassed both of them, and would explain their initial reluctance to consummate the marriage. Effie wrote to her mother, soon after the wedding, that her husband was 'the kindest creature in the world and takes a great deal of trouble in teaching me things.' She often described him as 'considerate', which was code for being undemanding in bed. And this was usually seen as a good thing. After all, it would have been hard for Effie to enjoy her travels in the Alps if she were in the early stages of pregnancy. In these first months, when she was visiting her parents in Scotland, Ruskin still wrote lovingly to his young wife, imagining their 'next bridal night', when 'I shall again draw your dress from your snowy shoulders, and lean my cheek upon them.' For him, Effie was ice-white, dangerous, like a glacier, 'soft, swelling, lovely, heavenly to the eye, but beneath there are winding clefts and dark places where men fall'.[150]

In the end, the lack of sex was only a small part of the problem. Lack of affection and compassion were the real issues, coupled with the interference of Ruskin's parents, which grew more poisonous as the years passed. Ruskin retreated into his books, spending more time in his study in his parents' house, and seeming relieved when Effie went home to Scotland for long holidays to help her mother.

There are at least two sides to the story of any marriage. Or in this case probably three or four, as the elder Ruskins and Grays were also very much involved, financially and emotionally. What we do know is that Ruskin's parents agreed to settle £10,000 on Effie, and paid for their married son's rented house and travel and art-buying habits. We also know that this meant they felt free to criticise Effie, as she was totally dependent on them, and Ruskin rarely stood up for her.

Perhaps this most private part of his history distracts us from the bigger story of Ruskin's writing, teaching and campaigning. It was only six years of his long career, and it is unedifying on all sides. Yet it shows the complicated reality of his experience, the disjunction between good intentions and the everyday difficulties of living and loving. It makes us question his fine words. He was a great thinker, prophetic almost, but a poor husband. Ruskin had never learnt to give way to anyone but his parents. He expected his wife to fit in with their patterns and his work. Maybe another woman would have submitted. But he had chosen a clever, high-spirited, independent girl, who sparkled in society but could never escape the censure of old Mr Ruskin. He was disappointed in his investment in this girl: 'She does not lead the Life I could have wished my Daughter-in-Law to lead.'[151] The marriage was an unsuccessful experiment which showed the limits of Ruskin's sensitivity. He was too inflexible, too bound up with his duty to his parents to adapt to married life. There was not enough love. As his father said, 'they never appeared to me to have more than a decent affection for each other, John being divided betwixt his wife and his pictures, and Phemy betwixt her Husband and her Dress.'[152]

In the end, Effie left the marriage untouched. And in her

own time. After a complicated summer staying in a tiny cottage in the Trossachs with the painter John Everett Millais and his brother, Effie finally confided in her parents. There was a lawsuit. Ruskin did not contest the case, and the marriage was annulled on the grounds of non-consummation. In his absence, Ruskin was declared incurably impotent. A year later, once the gossips had enjoyed their fill of the story, Effie and Millais were married. They went on to have eight children – Effie was pregnant within two months of her second wedding – and Ruskin and his parents tried to get on with their lives.

'Goodnight Rosie, Posie, Puss'

At the time, the legal decision seemed a small indignity to bear for the sake of being freed from his unloving marriage. But in the longer term, it blighted Ruskin's public name, and undermined his chances of marrying again more than a decade later, when he met Rose La Touche. There were several reasons why Rose was wary of engaging herself formally to the teacher she christened 'St. Crumpet'. Most of the time, she hesitated because of their religious differences. (She was a strict Evangelical Protestant, like Ruskin's mother, while he had become attracted to the possibilities of a more Catholic faith.) The age gap – twenty-nine years – was substantial, but does not seem to have been such a sticking point with her. For Rose's parents it was a problem, but the question of Ruskin's marriage to Effie was more troubling.

Rose's religious scruples, and her parents' anxieties about Ruskin's ability to love her as a husband should, led to years of indecision. Sometimes hopeful, sometimes hopeless, we read in Ruskin's diaries the awful seesawing emotions. He proposed formally when she was eighteen, but she made him wait three years for her answer – three years that scarred him. The date set for her answer, 'the 2nd of February became a great festival to me: now, like all the days of all the years, a shadow.'[153] For even then, she was not sure. Briefly in the late summer of 1872, he thought he had won her:

> (August 14, 1872.) – To-day came my consolation. I say 'to-day.' But it is two days past; for I could not write on the 14th, and scarcely since, for joy.
> (August 17.) – Oh me, that ever such thought and rest should be granted once more.
> (September 7.) – The ending day.
> (September 8.) – Fallen and wicked and lost in all thought; must recover by work.[154]

This was truly the ending of Ruskin's expectation that one day, somehow, they might be married. Rose had never been robust. But in her early twenties she became physically more fragile, and finally bedridden. Ruskin visited her. He drew her, and prayed with her, and briefly held her in his arms. Rose died in May 1875. She was twenty-six.

In some ways, he had lost the girl he had loved many

years before. She was constantly changing, he could never be sure of her. He had written to Georgie Burne-Jones as early as 1861, when Rosie was thirteen: 'I shall not see her till November.' Then he added: 'Nay, I shall never see *her* again. It's another Rosie every six months now. Do I want to keep her from growing up? Of course I do.'[155]

Perhaps Ruskin's desire to keep her young was one of the triggers for Rosie's ill-health. She seems to have suffered from an eating disorder. It may have been that she was trying to stop herself growing up, a desperate attempt to stay small and girlish, to remain loveable, and never have to make the hard decision about marriage. She would remain his 'little child-pet Rosie'.[156] From the very earliest days of their relationship, Ruskin had been pleased that 'her affection takes ... the form of a desire to please me and make me happy in any way that she can.' Even then, he reassured his father that 'Rosie's illness has assuredly *nothing* to do with ... me'.[157]

By the time Rosie was fifteen, Ruskin was already mourning her: 'She was a marvellous little thing when she was younger but – which has been one of the things that have troubled me – there came on some overexcitement of the brain, causing occasional loss of consciousness, and now she often seems only half herself, as if partly dreaming.'[158] She was drifting into puberty, and away from him. They both suffered, and Ruskin never fully recovered from her death – but Rosie suffered most. From the moment he singled her out, she was placed in an impossible position. He loved Rosie for her sweetness, her pert replies, her soft scolding. But, however hard she tried, she would always fail him. She could not remain the clear-eyed ten-year-old who had chatted with him as he taught her to draw.

'Joanna's care'

Rose La Touche's death was 'the seal of a great fountain of sadness which can now never ebb away'. The 'distracting and useless pain' remained with Ruskin to the end.[159] He did however, in his last decades, find a companionable relationship, one that sustained him, and gave him the laughter of little children in his home. It was not untroubled – as Ruskin became unwell, there were bitter arguments and temporary estrangements. But for many years he enjoyed a strange kind of quiet cousinly love, one that reassured him because it reminded him of the earliest affection he had enjoyed with Jessie and his Scottish kin.

After the sudden death of his father in March 1864, Ruskin and his mother were both hard hit. Mrs Ruskin, in particular, 'had been for so many years in every thought dependent on my father's wishes, and withdrawn from all other social pleasure as long as she could be his companion' that she had few friends, and was lonely.[160] She was also extremely set in her ways. Yet again, a young relative was brought into the Ruskin family, someone who would be grateful for a secure home, someone who had few other prospects. This time it

135

was Joan Agnew, a cousin from Wigtown in Scotland, who came to stay for a week when Ruskin had to go away for a short research trip, and who never left. Even after she married the artist Arthur Severn, her home was still with Ruskin. She cared for him, in sickness and in health, until the end.

Ruskin wrote about her with great warmth. His description of bringing her into the family home at Denmark Hill sounds oddly like a groom welcoming his bride at the altar: 'I very thankfully took her hand out of her uncle's, and received her in trust . . . I put her into my father's carriage at the door, and drove her out to Denmark Hill.' Joan was seventeen years old and, according to Ruskin, 'entirely nice'. She 'had real faculty and genius in all rightly girlish directions'. A young woman who had suffered many bereavements, she was brought into a grieving family. But she could sing, and read aloud, and dance. For once, Ruskin found her lovelier as she grew older: 'I think her a great deal prettier now than I did then . . . I am certain that everybody *felt* the guileless and melodious sweetness of her face.'

Joan was the woman that Ruskin had been waiting for all his life. She treated him sometimes like a child, sometimes as her master. She worked with him, sorting his collections of mineral samples, talking in her soft Scots voice, 'with busy pleasures for every hour.'[161] He never seems to have had any thought of marrying her – he was too bound up in his fascination with Rosie. But, when he was orphaned, they made a home together at Brantwood. Joanie, Arthur, and their five children expanded into the cottage by the lakeside. Ruskin sat in his study, when he was in good spirits, or she sat by his bedside when he was raving. Her kindly love sustained him. It was not always straightforward. No relationship lasting thirty-six years can be that simple. But, when he wrote about his past, his *Praeterita*, she was there alongside his loves: Jessie, Adèle and Rose of course. (Effie is passed over. Their marriage is not mentioned at all.) His Joanie gets a chapter all her own: the last chapter, 'Joanna's Care', patched together, and rambling, written just as the darkness closed in utterly.

Chapter 6

Losing

The Tomb of Ilaria del Caretto in the Duomo, Lucca

It is very strange to me to feel all my life become a thing of the past, and to be now merely like a wrecked sailor, picking up pieces of his ship on the beach. This is the real state of things with me, of course, in a double sense – People gone – and things. My Father and Mother, and Rosie, and Venice, and Rouen – all gone; but I can gather bits up of the places for other people.[162]

Ruskin is buried at the far end of Coniston churchyard, with a memorial like an ancient standing stone, carved with Celtic interlace. It looms above the simple crosses of the neighbouring graves, covered in strange and complex patterns that don't quite sit together: an angel, a menorah, a winged lion, an artist drawing the setting sun. As an attempt to synthesise Ruskin's life and enthusiasms, it falls short. By 1900, when he died, Ruskin's legacy was already too multi-faceted to be squeezed onto his headstone. There are no hopeful words about resurrection or reuniting. Ruskin lies alone until the angel lifts the trumpet to his lips to sound the end of all things.

I have been thinking about the flowers Ruskin would have hoped to find placed by his graveside. At his funeral, his friend, the artist George Frederic Watts, sent a wreath of laurel from his garden. I know that other visitors left primroses, for his Rosie. Or a stem of his favourite paradise lilies – he called them St Bruno's lilies – small and white among the golden leaves. But they only grow in the Alps. A few harebells for his little Scottish cousins? Or blue asphodels, with a 'spire two feet high, of more than two hundred stars, the stalks of them all deep blue, as well as the flowers', which he found on his father's birthday in 'the fields beyond Monte Mario'?[163] Perhaps a pot of dianthus, like the one in Ruskin's favourite picture of St Ursula. That would also be right for Rosie. As he struggled to retain his sanity, the real little Irish girl and the painted saint become one in his dreams.

On Christmas Day 1876, he wrote from Venice: 'Last night, St. Ursula sent me her dianthus "out of her bedroom window, with her love".' He went on, 'I was standing beside it, this morning, – (ten minutes ago only, – it has just struck eight), watching the sun rise out of a low line of cloud, just midway between the domes of St. George and the Madonna of Safety.'[164] There is a blurring of his understanding, and the convolutions of Ruskin's writing turn in on themselves.

Ruskin loved gathering flowers and sprigs of trees, writing about them, studying their tentative beauties. 'My right work,' he wrote, 'is to be out among the budding banks and hedges, outlining sprays of hawthorn and clusters of primrose.'[165] Every day when he was travelling with his parents, he would collect a small bunch of leaves on his morning walk, and set to drawing them, while his father read aloud. A discipline. A connection with his youth. For Ruskin each bloom or branch had a web of associations, some linguistic – like all the games he played with Rosie's name – while others were tied to a precious place or person. With deliberate echoes of Dante and his Beatrice, Ruskin was able to construct layers of a loving relationship with his dear girl, even when she was dead. Or perhaps, more imaginatively, more wholeheartedly when she was dead. Losing Rosie let him love her more fully.

Ruskin's joys were tinged with melancholy and nostalgia. He wanted to retain and share the most delicate pleasures, like the gentians he gathered and posted home to his Joanie on his last visit to Switzerland in 1882.[166] But often he felt helpless. He lost so much. His memoirs at times read like a litany of friends and family who died before they grew up. There are far too many dead young girls. And then he lost his court case against the painter James Whistler, which in turn undermined his standing as the preeminent art critic of his generation. And finally, after a decade of bereavement, he lost his mind. He always felt that he was swimming upstream. At the end, he was overwhelmed.

The day he found Joanie's gentians was one of the last good days, when he could walk high into the Alps, and set down his ideas clearly on paper. His editors, Cook and Wedderburn, described this as 'a last gleam'. He lived on for more than ten years, but by the end of the 1880s, he could no longer write in a straight line. The chapter he wanted to dedicate to Joanie wanders away, into reminiscences of Carlyle and strawberries, then to the coastline of Dumfries and Galloway, Sir Walter Scott's accent and blind fiddlers, and back towards Joan again, via 'the fishermen and ocean Gods of Solway, or the marchmen and mountain Gods of Cheviot',[167] her dancing and her beautiful singing voice, and, with a brief detour to walk in his garden with Rosie, eventually he brings us to meet Joan's future father-in-law in his studio overlooking the Trevi Fountain. We try to follow the winding paths of his memory. His mind is filled with names and places all connected somehow. But it is hard for us to enter his world now. There are flashes of colour and reason and bright sights, and then a knot that cannot be untangled, and he loses us too. 'How things bind and blend themselves together!' he wrote towards the end.[168]

'The ford of a dark river'

Of all Ruskin's loves, only Joanie outlived him. Even Effie died before him, not that he would have mourned her. The young women who briefly flicker into focus in the pages of his diaries or *Praeterita* are, all too often, dead before the end of the chapter. Drowning, childbirth, 'decline', 'very slowly of water on the brain'.

There is one, Charlotte Withers, who stays long enough to be described as a 'fragile, fair, freckled, sensitive slip of a girl about sixteen; graceful in an unfinished and small wild-flower sort of a way, extremely intelligent, affectionate, wholly right-minded, and mild in piety'. But she is also gone within a few paragraphs: 'A little while afterwards, her father "negotiated" a marriage for her with a well-to-do Newcastle trader, whom she took because she was bid. He treated her pretty much as one of his coal sacks, and in a year or two she died.'[169] I would like to know more about Charlotte and her sufferings. She was the only girl who appreciated Ruskin writing essays in her honour, and didn't laugh at him. Or perhaps he can only recreate her brief life in these short sentences because it was brief. If she had gone on to have a full and happy maturity, would Ruskin have remembered her? Would he have offered us this glimpse of a girl, if he knew she had become a grandmother? It is unlikely.

The ephemeral loveliness of young women, like flowers that bloom and fade, was a constant theme of Ruskin's writing. His memories of his cousin Jessie are bound up with gleanings from the cornfields, and foxgloves as well as harebells, and these remained after she passed 'the ford of a dark river' as her mother had foreseen in a 'simple and plain' dream, and 'there was no more Jessie'.[170]

These deaths are aestheticised and elided with the ebbing and flowing of the seasons. The girls almost become a *millefleurs* background to the tapestry of his life. But other losses were harder. How to survive his father? His sudden death in 1864 could not be reimagined in a dreamscape. The dreams did not come. Ruskin shared the raw aftermath of his bereavement with his friend Edward Burne-Jones. In some ways, he said, the finality of sitting with his father's body was better than the dragging uncertainties of his love for Rosie, and her fragile health. 'I'm used to live in pain, and this kind of pain does not kill by withering as other sorts of pain do; I have no feeling of weakness, nor of fever, and slept without dreaming last night – though the last forty hours were enough to make one dream, one should have thought.' And the next day: 'I find a curious thing that natural sorrow does not destroy strength, but gives it; while an irregular, out-of-way avoidable sorrow kills.' [171] The gnawing unhappiness of hopeless love, he found, was far worse than the shattering blow of losing his father. But the combination of these events was eventually too much. In the mid-1870s the hooks and eyes of his mind begin to unfasten.

He had been startlingly honest about his strained relationship with his father, and the conflicted emotions he experienced after his death. He tried to explain to his doctor that his father 'would have sacrificed his life for his son, and yet forced his son to sacrifice his life to him, and sacrifice it in vain.'[172] Ruskin felt at a loss, entirely dependent on his parents for money, and yet, it seemed, with nothing to show for it, except a fine collection of Turner watercolours. John James never saw his son become Slade Professor at Oxford. They had fallen out over Ruskin's radical social and political criticism in *Unto the Last*. And his romantic entanglements were best forgotten.

'Strange and sorrowful'

At the time, Ruskin seemed to weather that storm. But gradually he began to feel more unsettled and apologised to his readers that

> my head certainly does not serve me as it did once in many respects. The other day, for instance, in a frosty morning at Verona, I put on my dressing-gown (which is of bright Indian shawl stuff) by mistake for my great-coat; and walked through the full market-place, and half-way down the principal street, in that costume, proceeding in perfect tranquillity until the repeated glances of unusual admiration bestowed on me by the passengers led me to investigation of the possible cause.[173]

The 'long Dream' – days and nights teeming with hallucinations – caught up with him at last. In the delirium of madness, Ruskin fixed on the 'terrific impression of my failure in duty to my Father, and of the pain I had caused him, and my best friends'.[174] He came to grief after the deaths of his mother (1871) and Rose (1875). There was a first serious illness when he was staying at Matlock in the summer of 1871. Ruskin swore and raged and refused to listen to his doctors. He recovered his equilibrium, but then in 1878, he went 'heartily and headily mad'.

He tried to describe it to Thomas Carlyle, the man he called his 'papa': 'the most provoking and disagreeable of the spectres was developed out of the firelight on my mahogany bedpost; and my fate, for all futurity, seemed continually to turn on the humour of dark personages who were materially nothing but the stains of damp on the ceiling'. This time, the nature of the hallucinations had changed. At Matlock, even though his friends had felt he was in danger, his illness had in some ways energised him, had made him feel closer to the loved ones who were out of reach. But these new episodes were horrifying. They 'broke [him] all to pieces'.[175] Ruskin became paranoid. We can walk beside him as he documents his descent into despair in his diaries. And then we watch with his doctors and with Joan as the raving begins, and the accusations, and the anger, and agonising self-scrutiny.

It begins with physical and mental exhaustion. As he wrote to Charles Eliot Norton, his American friend, 'when I am tired I *can* neither draw nor think – and am simply forced to out of doors and dig – or prune – at least'.[176] Working in his garden, clearing and chopping wood does settle him.

But then the weather closes in. '[January 24, 1878] Thursday Awake since ¼ to 3 with the most hellish – frantic, terrific wind I've ever listened to, the climax of two days and nights perpetual black with sleet – one gleam of watery sunset for five seconds.'[177] Ruskin is left in 'a depression of my total me – body and soul, – not in any great sadness, but in a mean, small-withered way'. He still keeps up his correspondence. When letters arrive, he receives them as 'a most solemn kindness. I never needed it more'. He writes back that he is now in 'a stony and cold – or worse – muddy and poisoned – state of mind'. A day later he is 'down in dreamy scatterment and bewilderment'.[178]

It is still essential for Ruskin to record what he sees and the intellectual problems he is trying to solve. But he wakes before dawn, and 'all the calling names came into my head . . . I must put it all down as fast as I can.' But it makes no sense now. Jottings and memories: 'Usury & the pigs head and why I changed – Today if Ye will hear his voice – Oh me – and the seal on Chalcedony – and the Kettle and Geysers and boiling over and not boiling – I got all that too – besides the names this morning.' By the evening, his mind has calmed a little, and he can sit 'in my study with St Ursula in front of me, the token snowdrops – violets, maidenhair fern, and fleur-de-lys'.[179] Early spring flowers and St Ursula (Rose's alter ego) allow him to refocus.

Next day is worse.

Messages one after another crowding in – so fast – so fast – so innumerably ... Polly put the kettle on ... Flo – Flo – Flo – Telegraph Post – Talk about Astrology and Horace ... Ever so much more – which I must not stop now to remember – but try the Spirits whether they be with God, with patience ... Dreadfully tired, but trying to do everything decently and in order.[180]

Decently and in order. He was straining to hold on to his sanity. Two days later, he remembers a message from Rosie, saying 'I would serve her to the death'. And then he begins to write a litany of artists and poets, as if conjuring them, imploring them to come to his aid.

Burne-Jones – Oh my Black Prince
... Joseph Severn – Keats – Endymion
... And – you dear Blake – and so mad too –
Do you know what Titians good for now you stupid
  thing? ...
If only you would go barefoot a bit in the streets So
  pretty – so pretty.
Naked foot that shines like snow – and falls on earth
  – or gold – as mute ...
Tell me all about it – Raphael dead – from the angle
  then – and please angel of the lagoons from the
  Paradise – tell me what my own sweet Tintoret
  meant by those – Yes ...

150

(And praise be to thee – oh God. We praise thee Oh
   God, we acknowledge thee to be our Lord.)[181]

And the Dream engulfs him, violent, exhausting. He stays
awake all that cold night, stripped naked, to wrestle with the
Devil. 'Walking and waiting and watching, my mind racked
with ecstasy and anguish.' Just before dawn there is a struggle,
and 'a dull thud'. And nothing more.[182]

Ruskin's mental disturbances have never been fully diag-
nosed. This time, he suffered months of mania, refusing to
eat, paranoid, terrified, as he said, of shadows. His doctor
described his behaviour to Gladstone. He couldn't recognise
his friends, and 'He *raves* in the same clear voice and exquisite
inflection of tone, the most unmeaning words – modulating
them now with sweet tenderness, now with fierceness like
a chained eagle'.[183] Joan was hit hardest. She nursed him
through his stubborn madness, although 'it is so difficult *not
to mind* when he speaks in a calm deliberate voice, accusing
me of the most dreadful things! Saying he *knows* I am the
cause of all this – & through *me* he has been poisoned – &
he is lying dead in his coffin'.[184]

Ruskin claimed later that it was nothing to do with the
pressures of writing and lecturing. He believed long suffering
had caused his breakdown. It is hard to be clear about medical
causes at this distance. Perhaps Ruskin was experiencing the
early stages of dementia. Some forms of dementia can cause
sudden deterioration, and aggressive personality changes.

But between the upsetting and disruptive episodes, Ruskin was able to regain his equilibrium. If it were any other nineteenth-century artistic figure, we would ask, is this syphilis? Some of his symptoms – delusions, melancholia, impaired judgement and concentration, self-blame – resemble the 'paralytic dementia' associated with the disease, which can appear up to thirty years after infection. However, Ruskin never showed any signs of the skin complaints or blindness which usually accompany the infection. And, of course, he was celibate – as far as we know.

Is it possible that his hypersensitivity to visual experience might be related to his later ill-health? At times he really does seem to be able to see more intensely, exploring a painting or a landscape with his eyes in a way that makes the rest of us seem half blind. Occasionally people who have suffered strokes can be left with altered perception. They become more aware of colours and visual details, and can take great pleasure in this newness of vision.

I learnt of this possibility when talking to a stroke survivor. We were on an art tour of Tuscany, and standing on a terrace, watching the sun set over Florence. He described an extraordinary world of visual beauty that had opened up to him in the wake of his stroke – colours were more vivid, greens beyond anything he'd known before. He had simply fallen in love with looking. (At the same time, he said, his musical ear had been deadened, and his favourite pieces now sounded harsh. His whole sense perception had been shaken.) Suddenly, it seemed that this might be one way of explaining Ruskin's clear-sightedness. If he was experiencing strokes, would this account for the sudden onset of his traumatic 'Dreams', as he described them? Whatever the cause, the distress was real, long-lasting, and affected not only Ruskin, but all his carers who bore the brunt of his anger and unreason.

In his own mind, the crises were associated with the loss of his parents, and of Rose. He had nightmares about quarrelling with his mother, daydreams of conversations with Rosie. They all contributed to his disquiet. And then there is the list of fellow artists that he summons to his aid. At the head of that list was Edward Burne-Jones. Ruskin needed his friend at this moment because he was scared. He was going to be put on trial, and would be expected to account for his words, his outspoken opinions. He hoped that Burne-Jones would stand with him. The troubles of 1878 are all bound up with this public humiliation. James Whistler, who knew how to handle a rhetorical flourish just as brilliantly as Ruskin, was taking the critic to court. And Burne-Jones was called upon to defend him.

'Flinging a pot of paint in the public's face'

Throughout the 1870s, Ruskin had been writing *Fors Clavigera*, his sporadic 'Letters to the workmen and labourers of Great Britain'. It was a spontaneous and wide-ranging

153

series of 'think pieces', often responding to something news-worthy or personal. His style was conversational, moving swiftly from one concern to the next – economics, literature, foreign policy, art – they all came under his scrutiny.

In the summer of 1877, a new art gallery opened its doors. The Grosvenor Gallery was designed as 'a palace of art', with works shown by invitation only. It was a shop window for more advanced painters, who found the Royal Academy too stultifying.

Ruskin missed the opening. He was coming home from Venice, and was not quite himself. When he did review the show, he singled out Burne-Jones for particular praise. His *Days of Creation* designs were not perfect, but Burne-Jones was mentioned in the same breath as 'Giotto, Masaccio, Luini, Tintoret, and Turner'. Whistler, on the other hand, was a charlatan, who was asking 'two hundred guineas for flinging a pot of paint in the public's face'. His display, especially his *Nocturne in Black and Gold: the Falling Rocket*, was an act of 'ill-educated conceit' and 'wilful imposture'.[185] In Ruskin's opinion, Whistler's *Nocturne* was a hasty sketch, dressed up in a gold frame, and offered as a finished work of art. Anyone who bought it was being conned. It was not worth the money.

It was not the first time that Ruskin had attacked Whistler. In a lecture of October 1873, he had described one of Whistler's pictures as 'a daub', something 'which had taken about a quarter of an hour to scrawl'.[186] But this latest taunt was too much. *Fors* had a wide readership and Ruskin's reviews could still make or break an artist's career.

Whistler was a perfectionist; each sweep of the brush was carefully choreographed. He believed that paintings 'should be like the breath on the surface of a pane of glass'. The swift and spontaneous appearance of his works was, like many things he touched, an elaborate construct, a pose. He loved the suggestion of changefulness in his pictures of flowing water or falling fireworks. This was a new art, a fresh, modern manner, deliberately provocative. Whistler was going to make Ruskin suffer for his throwaway line. The two men never met face to face, but the repercussions of Ruskin's words, and Whistler's retaliation, shattered both their lives. Whistler moved fast, taking legal advice within days, and serving a summons for libel on 8 August.

This call to stand trial was painfully reminiscent of the end of Ruskin's marriage. Like Effie and the annulment, Whistler's legal challenge wrong-footed Ruskin. He had become accustomed to speaking his mind, and stirring. That was his self-appointed role, not just as an arbiter of taste, but increasingly as a commentator on working practices. He had reproached Whistler not because he couldn't paint, but because the painting appeared unfinished. It was slapdash.

Preparations for the court case formed the backdrop to Ruskin's deteriorating mental health. His collapse in the early spring of 1878 seems to have been partly the result of his anxiety about defending his opinions in the witness box.

That was why he cried out for Burne-Jones in his distress. He needed someone who understood that modern art could be both imaginatively bold and also highly finished. They had travelled together, fallen out and made up. Burne-Jones knew what mattered to Ruskin, and agreed to stand beside him at the trial.

The case came to court on 23 November 1878. Ruskin was described, in his absence, as holding 'perhaps the highest position in Europe or America as an art critic' but he had abused this position by suggesting 'that Mr Whistler is guilty of fraud in asking the price he has done'.[187]

Burne-Jones reluctantly agreed to appear to defend Ruskin. He saw Whistler's work as 'very incomplete. It is an admirable beginning ... It is masterly in some respects, especially in colour. It is a beautiful sketch ... [but] It is deficient in form, and form is as essential as colour.' When he was asked, 'Is it, in your opinion, a work of art?' Burne-Jones replied, 'No, I cannot say that it is. It would be impossible to call it a serious work of art ... This is only one of a thousand failures that artists have made in their efforts at painting night.'[188]

Burne-Jones soon regretted his statement. At the time, he felt he had to speak on Ruskin's behalf: his friend was still so ill. But he hated being in the public eye, and believed he had been pushed into a corner, and made to sound old-fashioned and insensitive. He was an artist, not a critic. It put a strain on their relationship. And it was all pointless.

Ruskin lost the case. But Whistler did not fare much

better. He was only awarded a farthing in damages, and was driven to bankruptcy, because of the legal costs – losing his house and his position as a portraitist. He spent a long, achingly cold winter in Venice. Whistler had signed his works with a flourish, turning his initials into a butterfly with a sting in his tail. But for a while, his carefully choreographed career was blown off course.

For the wider art world, the repercussions of this verdict rippled beyond the nineteenth century, and into the birth of modernism. We can point to this moment in 1878, when an artist says 'this is a work of art', and that is enough. Tests of skill or subject no longer count. Put a urinal on a pedestal, or rumpled bed sheets on a gallery floor, or sit in the street wearing a sign saying 'Look at me': all these are finished works, because the artist tells us so.[189] In Whistler vs. Ruskin, we can see the origins of Dada, *Arte Povera* and performance art. The judge decided that it is the intention of the creator that matters, not the response of the critic or patron.

For Ruskin, the verdict was a dreadful blow. His authority was held against him. He lost his position as the voice of the radical in art. Where was his open-heartedness, his clear sight now? He had shown that he was out of step with the sophisticated, sensitive, 'subjectless' works being exhibited in the Grosvenor Gallery. His mental fragility meant that, for the time being, he was no match for the razor-sharp wit of Whistler. In the weeks leading up to Christmas 1878, Ruskin remained withdrawn. After the verdict, he explained that 'the weather has most grievously depressed me this last week, and I have not been fit to speak to anybody'. He wrote to a few friends, about bird's nests and coloured crystals, but mostly he found 'these grey skies are mere poison to my thoughts'.[190]

'The Storm-Cloud of the Nineteenth Century'

The sun remained behind the clouds for month after month. Ruskin's depression rarely lifted. He resigned his professorship at Oxford, and watched the skies. Where was the brightness, where were the soft rains he remembered? The weather seemed to be changing, and he mourned the loss of the glorious sunsets he had once painted. He tried to hold on to them, the 'threads, and meshes, and tresses, and tapestries' of ice clouds above the Old Man of Coniston, 'flying, failing, melting, reappearing; spinning and unspinning themselves, coiling and uncoiling, winding and unwinding, faster than eye or thought can follow ... emerald and ruby and pale purple and violet melting into a blue that is not of the sky, but of the sunbeam'.[191]

Ruskin saw the world was darkening. It was partly his internal turbulence – he recognised that. But it was something more, something related to pollution in the air. He began to notice it in the early 1870s, when he was staying in Derbyshire, just before his first episode of insanity. It was midsummer but, he wrote, 'the sky is covered with grey cloud; – not rain-cloud, but a dry black veil, which no ray of sunshine can pierce ... and everywhere the leaves of the trees are shaking fitfully ... to show the passing ... of a strange, bitter, blighting wind.' It was very troubling, a dreadful and permanent alteration in the weather patterns. It was man-made, and was the result of poor stewardship. 'Blanched Sun, – blighted grass, – blinded man.' He called it blasphemy, this destruction of the 'Earth, as prepared for the abode of man', through a combination of 'idleness, folly, and vice'.[192] When we hear his voice now, he sounds uncomfortably like a thundering preacher. But that is because the message is uncomfortable. And prescient.

Ruskin did not coin the phrase 'climate change', but he knew it was happening. He tried to raise awareness by his lec-turing. He saw the effect of these changes on our well-being and our environment. He quoted a letter from a friend who had noticed that 'neither the look of the sky nor the character of the weather has been, as we should say, what it used to be'.[193] He was not alone in trying to raise the alarm. Fears about smog and the polluted Thames in the 'Great Stink' had made headlines since the 1850s and '60s. 'Pea-soupers' caused disease and accidents, and fear of what might happen in the dark. But Ruskin showed the problem was not local. Effluent from factories and homes flowed into the air and water supplies, and reached beyond the city, tainting the meadows and clouds and sea. One of the reasons Ruskin objected to Whistler's *Nocturnes* was because they made the chimneys and slag heaps of Battersea look beautiful. Ruskin could see no loveliness in the enveloping soot-laden smog.

His descriptions of the impact of human behaviour, the importance of individual choices, and our personal responsibility ring very true today. If we keep our eyes lowered and refuse to look about us, we can pretend not to notice. He showed us that we must look more closely, question commercial and industrial practices, and think about our waste. He warned us. The Technicolor waves of plastic in the far oceans would horrify him, but not surprise him. He had tried to raise the alarm. But the encroaching 'Storm Cloud', which seemed to intensify after the trial, threw him off kilter.

Ruskin recognised the impact of human actions on climate and the landscape. He knew our need for green spaces. Gardening, and walking in the Alps and in Scotland, were essential for his own mental health. But his observations went beyond the personal. In the course of his travels, he became aware of the dreadful consequences of cutting down trees. He had spotted that 'roots bind together the ragged edges of rocks . . . so that, while it is always dangerous to pass under a treeless edge of an overhanging crag, as soon as it has become beautiful with trees, it is safe also.' He goes on: 'By cutting down forests on great mountain slopes, not only is the climate destroyed, but the danger of superficial landslip fearfully increased.'[194] His constant attention to detail, looking up and looking under, meant that he understood the complex repercussions of deforestation.

He had watched in misery over many years, as he realised that the glaciers of his youth were also in retreat. With industrialisation reaching the foothills of the Alps, air pollution was now visible. And so was the impact of climate change on the great rivers of ice. In May 1869, he wrote despairingly of the tainted atmosphere: 'the air which once inlaid the clefts of all their golden crags with azure is now defiled with languid coils of smoke, belched from worse than volcanic fires'. He went on: 'Their very glacier waves are ebbing, and their snows fading, as if Hell had breathed on them ... These are no careless words – they are accurately – horribly – true ... The light, the air, the waters, all defiled!'[195] Losing the snows and the sunshine, fearing to lose the forests: these anxieties fuelled his descent into madness. There was too much to do, and he felt like he was never going to be heard. No one seemed to see the urgency. He was trying to find ways to fix the world, and instead

all my friends are throwing stones through my window, and dropping parcels down the chimney, and shrieking through the keyhole that they must and will see me instantly, and lying in wait for me if I want a breath of fresh air, to say their life depends on my instantly superintending the arrangements of their new Chapel, or Museum, or Model Lodging-house, or Gospel steam-engine. And I'm in such a fury at them all that I can scarcely eat ... In Heaven's name, *be quiet* just now![196]

There was no peace. He fell silent.

Chapter 7
Working

Chamonix. Mer de Glace, Mont Blanc Massif

It matters little, ultimately, how much a labourer is paid for making anything; but it matters fearfully what the thing is, which he is compelled to make. If his labour is so ordered as to produce food, and fresh air, and fresh water, no matter that his wages are low; – the food and fresh air and water will be at last there; and he will at last get them. But if he is paid to *destroy* food and fresh air, or to produce iron bars instead of them, – the food and air will finally *not* be there, and he will *not* get them, to his great and final inconvenience.

I have long been accustomed . . . to hear my statements laughed at for years . . . They will forthwith tell you that 'what you say is very beautiful, but it is not practical'.[197]

It is springtime in the Black Country. I am travelling again with Ruskin in mind. This time I'm heading for Ruskin Land

– a curious, semi-wild place, that sounds like a theme park – but I'll explain more in a moment when I reach the turning. For now, I'm still on the road, contemplating Ruskin's reactions to the world beyond my windscreen. Queen Anne's lace persists on the edge of the lane, the surging white dancing among the green. And then, a bank of late bluebells. There are pennants of plastic in the hedgerows, the remnants of shopping bags, orange and scarlet, caught on the blackthorn. I am implicated in this tidal wave of plastic too. I remembered to stuff my refillable coffee cup into my holdall before I left the house, but I count three half-filled water bottles in the car, plus the crumpled gold sweetie wrappers. Where will they go in the long run?

The satnav is taking me on a rat run through the back lanes, over speed bumps designed to slow down the 4 x 4s. The car in front takes extra care – her bumper sticker says 'Cake on board', and she doesn't want to crack the icing. A commuter train crosses the blackened brick arches of a viaduct, pulling towards Birmingham. Now the road is raised, lifting me to the height of the tree canopies, the leaves dusty and discoloured alongside the flyover.

I imagine Ruskin in the passenger seat, as I become increasingly aware of the intersections between his writings and our responsibilities. His fears for our well-being were well founded. He asked the difficult questions. How do we look after our land? How should we earn our living? He thought about consumption, pollution, capitalism, responsibility. He showed us alternatives – utopias or fairy tales perhaps, but still worth contemplating.

I enter the next town, labelled 'Fair Trade' on its outskirts. Does it make a difference? Three old men wait outside a church, dressed in overcoats and their funeral ties. Across the road, there is a small business with a sign promising 'Integrity and Service since 1831'. I am reminded of Ruskin's epitaph for his own father, the best he could say of him. Not 'loving' or 'generous', but 'honest'. Ruskin told his readers that he had 'written on the granite slab over his grave that he was "an entirely honest merchant"'.[198] This was the spirit in which Ruskin was brought up: unsentimental, and hard-working. It was also the source of his constant sense of failure. Ruskin lived on the proceeds of his father's work, and earned precious little from his own writing or lecturing. All his travels, his houses, his enthusiasms, his Turner paintings, even his melancholy – he owed them all to his father. Neither of them could ever forget this debt. Ruskin gave away what he could, making donations of money and pictures, of his time and his energy, until he was exhausted. But even here, outside Bewdley, the piece of ground that bears his name was bought by a friend.

Ruskin Land

I am nearly there, still with snatches of his writings buzzing inside my head. The roads are quieter, and now I begin my approach along a narrow lane that becomes a rutted track. I go slowly, and wind down the windows. I pass an old cherry orchard and a row of beehives. Up between the oaks and pine trees I can see St George's Farm, and a little bungalow with a child's swing in the garden. At the heart of the Wyre forest there is an unpicturesque clearing, with a couple of long low sheds, open to the hard-stand. And a Portakabin. And the sound of a chainsaw in the distance. This is a working farm, a productive land for timber and fruit. There is space for a blacksmith, and a herd of black Dexter beef cattle.

Young people from the city come here to learn woodworking skills, making useful things from the green timber. They press the apples for cider. They testify to the peace they find here. The staff, young or old, are kind and positive. Practical, handy. They pass me a battered OS map, with Ruskin Land clearly marked, and point out the stream on the edge of their patch. I'm hoping to make sound recordings for an exhibition to celebrate Ruskin's birthday. Visitors to the art gallery will perhaps hear my footfalls on the crackling bracken, or the flutter of goldfinches over the yard, or moving water. It seems one simple way to bring the experience of this place to a wider audience, to overlay the paintings with an almost imperceptible dusting of outdoor sound, the things we take for granted as we walk through the woods. In my headphones, I hear the beating of birds' wings in the apple trees, and the regular rasping of a plane on an oak board.

Ruskin Land is an extraordinary place, inelegant and

effective. Working outdoors in the sawmill; coppicing the ancient forest to encourage new plants to fill the gaps between the great stands of trees; using the grazing lands for sustainable husbandry – these are all offshoots of Ruskin's writings, and are clearly beneficial to the land and to its people. This is Ruskin in action. It can be done, on a small scale. It is hard work, and doesn't pay much. You'll go home with sore hands and frozen feet. But families have been settling here since before the Great War, and the project is still thriving. Not all of the orchards of damsons and pears have survived, but in recent years the woodlands and meadows have been restored. It is still run by Ruskin's philanthropic trust, the Guild of St George, which also owns the art collection in Sheffield. Art, handcraft and environmental stewardship are all brought together under the banner of this organisation.

'Prickly independence'

Ruskin turned his attention to political economy – essentially the best way to work – increasingly in the 1860s. The more he looked at beautiful buildings, the more he wanted to understand the shape of the society that created them. Architecture, especially Gothic architecture, seemed to be key to this understanding. It was the meeting point of hand skills, political aspirations, faith and technology. Ruskin wanted to see how they fitted together, and how modern industrialising societies might learn to transform themselves into something more humane.

It was a shock to his readers when he began to move from criticising paintings to criticising capitalism. He had been thinking in this way for years, ever since his analysis of the treatment of workers in *The Stones of Venice* (1853). For him, the carved capitals and crockets on a Gothic building reflected the workers' freedom of expression. Creative variety, and a fondness for natural ornament, lay at the heart of Ruskin's commentary on Venetian art and society. He pointed to the contrast with the rigid conformity of classical or Renaissance architecture, where symmetry seemed to be more important than the organic growth of a building. In his words,

> if, as in Greek work, all the capitals are alike, and all the mouldings unvaried, then the degradation is complete.[199]

Changefulness, Naturalism and Redundance (that is, 'the uncalculating bestowal of the wealth of its labour') were three of the characteristics of Gothic architecture that he identified. They all reflected the possibility for the worker to express 'a magnificent enthusiasm ... a profound sympathy with the fulness and wealth of the material universe'.[200] As Ruskin saw it, 'if, as in Gothic work, there is perpetual change both in design and execution, the workman must have been altogether set free.'[201] The close connection between an interest in the natural world and the ability to create beautiful works of art lay at the heart of this argument. It seemed that men in medieval Venice must have had time and opportunity to study plants, their leaf forms, the way they grew up and around, their strength as they swayed. Their architecture was informed by 'their peculiar fondness for the forms of Vegetation'.[202] Ruskin wrote that 'it was no chance suggestion of the form of an arch from the bending of a bough, but a gradual and continual discovery . . . [until] the stony pillar grew slender and the vaulted roof grew light, till they had wreathed themselves into the semblance of the summer woods.'[203] Looking closely at trees and flowers was an essential part of the creative process. Ruskin skated over the details of exactly who designed the various parts of a Gothic building, from the master mason to the hod carrier (who presumably had very little freedom of expression). But he encouraged his readers to recognise that workers benefit from contact with trees and green spaces. It lets them breathe, and helps them innovate.

Ruskin also knew that this element of freedom was lacking in the lives of many workers now. They no longer had access to fields or woods, to growing things. They were increasingly constrained by the industrialised landscapes of Britain, and their opportunity for self-expression at work was almost nil. His study of *The Stones of Venice* began with his fascination with the fourteenth century, but at key moments he brought the modern working world back into focus.

In particular, he questioned the necessity of the 'division of labour', arguing that

> It is not, truly speaking, the labour that is divided; but the men: – Divided into mere segments of men – broken into small fragments and crumbs of life; so that all the little piece of intelligence that is left in a man is not enough to make a pin, or a nail, but exhausts itself in making the point of a pin or the head of a nail.

As Ruskin saw it, the factory system failed the workers. It did not make their lives brighter, nor educate their children, nor improve the quality of their drinking water. His words overflowed, using all the rhetorical dexterity he had learnt listening to his Sunday sermons as a child. He left his readers with an almost apocalyptic vision as:

> the great cry that rises from all our manufacturing cities, louder than their furnace blast, is all in very deed for this, – that we manufacture everything there except men; we blanch cotton, and strengthen steel, and refine sugar, and shape pottery; but to brighten, to strengthen, to refine, or to form a single living spirit, never enters into our estimate of advantages.[204]

How was this system to be overturned? By education, and by the power of the consumer: 'It can be met only by a right understanding, on the part of all classes, of what kinds of labour are good for men, raising them, and making them happy; . . . and by equally determined demand for the products and results of healthy and ennobling labour.'[205]

Ruskin's political solutions often smack of paternalism. At times, he specifically suggests that an employer should imagine employees as their children, and for 'the master' to 'ask himself sternly whether he is dealing with such subordinate as he would with his own son'. When facing economic distress, Ruskin insists that a captain of industry should accept their own share of the misery, or 'even to take more of it for himself than he allows his men to feel; as a father would in a famine, shipwreck, or battles'.[206] There is a lot of autobiographical feeling bound up in his descriptions of the idealised merchant. Ruskin points out 'the merchant is presumed to act always selfishly'. However, 'the market may have its martyrdoms as well as the pulpit; and trade its heroisms.'[207] Ruskin's own father had brought his family sherry business back from bankruptcy, but he had always felt socially vulnerable because of his position as a middleman, buying and selling. Ruskin felt the stigma of growing up 'in trade'. It coloured his attitude to class, money and the market.

Of course, we will have many other legitimate concerns about Ruskin's ways of imagining the economic relationship between employers and worker – not just because of the bias of his own background. In his most influential articles on political economy, published as *Unto this Last* (1862), Ruskin writes exclusively about male bosses and male workers. He briefly mentions the difficulties of employing domestic servants – a female concern, both for the housemaid and her mistress. And he includes 'the housewife who takes care of her furniture in the parlour, and guards against all waste in the kitchen' in his list of people who add 'continually to the riches and well-being of the nation'.[208] But he barely registers the probability of women earning wages in the wider economy beyond the home. The factory workers, soldiers, pastors, doctors, merchants, farmers and idlers described in his parables are all men.

We may argue that Ruskin was using 'man' in the same way as the Authorised Version of the Bible, or the Book of Common Prayer does – to mean all people, male and female, young and old. We may point to his work with the girls' school at Winnington, or his open lectures to women to demonstrate his interest in female education. Or his encouragement of artists like Elizabeth Siddal and Kate Greenaway. But it is still a dreadful blind spot. Ruskin's ingrained masculine viewpoint has undermined his reputation as a modern political commentator.

However, his rejection of 'the market' as the best way to ensure fair wages and fair trade was radical. This was why readers like William Morris and Gandhi took *Unto this Last* as one of their texts for transforming society. His words generated fruitful discussions, opened up new viewpoints. They could be seen in a historical context. Or the ideals of the past could be translated into the present. That was how he became the godfather of the 'back to the land' movements, and green socialism. His suggestions informed Gandhi's rejection of empire and capitalism, and helped to shape the welfare state in Britain. Ruskin wrote across disciplines. His appeal comes very much from the open-ended proposals and colourful analogies he put forward in *Unto this Last* and *Fors Clavigera*, where he speaks personally and passionately. In his political writings, as in his art criticism, he leads us from the small-scale, the hand-held, to the grand sweeping gestures of a fire-and-brimstone preacher.

Ruskin was never affiliated to a political party. He could distance himself from the intricacies of delivering reform, as well as the day-to-day difficulties of having to run a business. He declared, for example, that he was not 'taking up, nor countenancing one whit, the common socialist idea of division of property' while also announcing that he was 'reddest of all the red'.[209] Occasionally he described himself as a 'violent Tory of the old school'.[210] This again was a deliberate decision to set himself apart from the reality of contemporary politics, and his antagonism towards the 'laissez-faire' approach of the Liberals. He was antagonistic to the instability of both systems – anarchy on one hand, the vicissitudes of the free market on the other. For Ruskin, 'Government and co-operation are in all things the Laws of Life; Anarchy and competition the Laws of Death.'[211]

Habits of labour and life

One of the first things he criticised was unstable employment. He was disheartened by the short-termism of many major employers, who would not guarantee regular wages. In effect, his words anticipate the anxieties caused by current 'zero-hours' contracts, or the 'gig economy' that relies on a pool of underemployed workers to fill the gaps. Ruskin knew that there was a need for a basic living wage, and anything less than that would be disastrous for a working family. 'Supposing that a man cannot live on less than a shilling a day,' he wrote, 'his seven shillings he must get, either for three days' violent work, or six days' deliberate work. The tendency of all modern mercantile operations is to throw both wages and trade into the form of a lottery.'[212] This model led, as Ruskin said, towards 'Anarchy and competition'. He suggested that the workers should be paid a lower day rate, but with more regular hours. Job security, he recognised, made a vast difference to the attitude of workers towards their labour.

And, from the outset, he pointed to the power of the cash in our pockets. As customers, we can demand better products. We can hold manufacturers responsible for the pay and conditions they offer their employees. We can lobby and ask the awkward questions, about the sources of raw materials or the carbon footprint of a product. Is it really acceptable to use child labour to stitch footballs? Or to ship our discarded shampoo bottles halfway around t̶... someone else to sift and recycle? How can we jus̶... choices as consumers? 'Fast fashion' and 'rock-bottom ... are a false economy: we might gain, personally, temporari̶... but someone else is bound to lose. As Ruskin put it:

> Whenever we buy or try to buy cheap goods ... remember we are stealing somebody's labour ... taking from him the proper reward of his work and putting it into your pocket. You know well enough that the thing could not have been offered you at that price, unless distress of some kind had forced the producer to part with it. You take advantage of this distress.

If we begin to recognise our place in the 'traffic' of goods and services, then we can start to take responsibility – check-ing labels, changing our shopping habits, supporting local suppliers, thinking about sustainability. In Ruskin's words, we should strive to 'waste nothing, and grudge nothing'. He wanted us to recognise 'that every atom of substance, of whatever kind, used or consumed, is so much human life spent'.[213] Who digs the earth to supply our food? Who weaves the fabric of our clothes? Who cleans up our mess? Ruskin returns again and again to the personal. He insists that we cannot treat our workers as simply 'covetous machines'. Emotions, affections, faith, family, hunger, these are the driv-ing forces for all employees. He described a labourer as 'an agine whose motive power is a Soul'.[214] Ruskin accepted that not everyone in his audience would believe in God or an afterlife. But it makes all the difference if we do or not. When we argue about the business of war, for example, do we imagine 'that a discharge of artillery would merely knead down a certain quantity of once living clay into a level line, as in a brickfield; or whether, out of every separately Christian-named portion of the ruinous heap, there went out, into the smoke and dead-fallen air of battle, some astonished condition of soul, unwillingly released'?[215]

What are the implications, if this life is all there is? For Ruskin, a just master and fair pay matter more when there is no Father in Heaven overseeing our travails. If workers cannot be promised a sweet eternity of rest, then the here-and-now needs to be pleasant and fulfilling. Ruskin reminded his readers that those who hold sway over money and power were answerable for the souls (if they had them) and bodies of the people they drag in their wake. In his mind, the biggest 'question for the nation is not how much labour it employs, but how much life it produces'.[216] Was it possible to change the systems of production and consumption, to enhance the lives of those at the bottom as well as those at the top? He needed to point out the iniquities as he saw them.

Ruskin attacked many of the underpinnings of the cap-italist structure, including the 'disgraceful ... commercial text, "Buy in the cheapest market and sell in the dearest"'.[217] This approach relied on taking advantage of other people's misfortunes. He was outraged by the principle of speculation – of money breeding money: 'Even in its best conditions,' he wrote, 'it is merely one of the forms of gambling or treasure-hunting.' His criticism was partly moralising. Ruskin could see no virtue in watching and waiting for someone else to fail, so that the bank could gain. He described those who hoarded money or goods as 'pools of dead water, and eddies in a stream', useless, stagnant.[218] Or like 'children trying to jump on the heads of their own shadows; the money-gain being only the shadow of true gain'.[219] He also knew that, as the markets rose and fell, there would be individual losers, people whose lives were devastated by the fluctuations in flow of capital. He asked, 'Have you ever deliberately set yourselves to imagine and measure the suffering, the guilt, and the mortality caused necessarily by the failure of any large-dealing merchant, or largely-branched bank?'[220] His concerns resonate for those of us still living with the after-effects of the Crash of 2008, and the new age of austerity. Savings, homes, small businesses, plans for retirement, were destroyed by the banking crises. This is what happens, according to Ruskin, when people 'cannot bear to let any opportunity of gain escape them, and frantically rush at every gap and breach in the walls of Fortune, raging to be rich'.[221]

Implementing the changes was never going to be easy. Ruskin was only one voice in a developing, multistranded conversation about the Labour movement. These debates covered land ownership, municipal and central government, voting rights, Cooperative and Building Societies, and were often linked to campaigns about Ireland, female emancipation, sexual politics and education. During his lifetime, the emergent Socialist groups in Britain were influenced more by Ruskin's writings, and by the Chartist and Utopian traditions of Robert Owen, than by Marx and Engels. Marxism was barely visible in Victorian Britain. Engels's study of industrial Manchester, *The Condition of the Working Class in England*, was translated into English in 1887. And Eleanor Marx, Karl's daughter and fellow radical, wrote regular articles for William Morris's Socialist magazine *Commonweal* from 1885. But these hardly made an impact until after 1900. Ruskin refers in passing to Marx's 'International Association of Working Men', founded in 1864. But he recognised that most of his readers would find his own critique of land ownership and capitalism too radical. He suggested that 'land should belong to those who can use it, and tools to those who can use them; or, as a less revolutionary, and instantly practicable, proposal, that those who have land and tools – should use them'.[222] In other words, the landowner should make his estate productive, and the capitalist should reinvest his income, creating livelihoods for workers. Ruskin's politics were always seen through the prism of the personal; he constructed his theories on the basis of enhanced relationships between the classes, by increased sympathy rather than 'the world turned upside down'. Local transformations, at parish level, not cataclysmic change.

Ruskin abhorred the idea of revolution or destruction. The horrors of French history, from 1789 and the Terror to the Commune of 1871, meant that he saw no hope in the unfettered power of 'the people'. He hoped for a more thoughtful response from the ruling classes – and he did believe that some were better able to rule than others. He longed for a change of heart, an almost Evangelical 'conversion' among those in authority, who would see that ruling for the many, not the few, was the right way to use their sovereignty. His political legacy in the twenty-first century has been rather quiet. Few Members of Parliament or local councillors today would name Ruskin as an inspiration. But, thanks to the breadth of his writings, his influence can be traced in the growth of Green activism as well as in women's education; the rise of the Labour Party and the idealism of the Liberal Democrats.

Ruskin recognised that for many people, especially comfortable middle-class people, the idea of shaking up the system was too disruptive. The status quo worked for them. Many would avoid committing themselves to the rigorous labour that Ruskin advocated: 'If you want knowledge, you must toil for it: if food, you must toil for it: and if pleasure, you must toil for it.'[223] He imagines his wealthy readers changing places with the working classes. How would they cope doing a tedious job on a minimum wage, with nothing to spare at the end of the week?

It would be well if we sometimes tried it practically ourselves, and spent a year or so at some hard manual labour, not of an entertaining kind – ploughing or digging, for instance, with a very moderate allowance of beer; nothing but bread and cheese for dinner; no papers nor muffins in the morning; no sofas nor magazines at night; one small room for parlour and kitchen; and a large family of children always in the middle of the floor.[224]

Ruskin sympathised, and did not expect too much of the working classes. Why should they be more temperate, more patient than people with bigger houses, and larger incomes?

But however much he talked about handwork and 'seven shillings a week', he could only play at being poor. His father had 'never spent more than half of his income', and as he was growing up, Ruskin 'had never seen a moment's trouble or disorder in any household matter; nor anything whatever either done in a hurry, or undone in due time'.[225] What would he really know about belt-tightening, and how would he manage 'if there is only a crust of bread in the house, and mother and children are starving'?[226] Unlike other commentators who raised awareness of workers' rights, he could only stand outside and look in through the window at the domestic difficulties of the poor. Ruskin acknowledged that Charles Dickens's work was particularly powerful and 'the things he tells us are always true'.[227] Dickens, of course, could speak from experience.

The gutter and the diggings

Ruskin's attempts at handwork (rather than brain work) were often more symbolic than practical. He claimed that 'the quite happiest bit of manual work I ever did was for my mother in the old inn' when they were travelling in Savoy. He washed down the stone staircase, bringing 'the necessary buckets of water from the yard myself'. Ruskin 'poured them into beautiful image of Versailles waterworks down the fifteen or twenty steps of the great staircase, and with the strongest broom I could find, cleaned every step into its corners. It was quite lovely work to dash the water and drive the mud, from each, with accumulating splash down to the next one.'[228]

This was work done for his mother and for his own pleasure. It was cleansing and dramatic, an attempt to recreate the cascades of Versailles in a hotel. He was at leisure, and he always loved the idea of waterworks. He does not record what the maids thought of his handiwork. It seems unlikely that they found it helpful – he was pointing out their failings, and making the place wet and slippery. But, for Ruskin, his mother's needs were more important than theirs. And he would be off in the travelling carriage within a day or two.

Ruskin's fascination with moving water persisted through his life. He tried several times, in his London home and in Brantwood, to design and build watercourses. As a boy, he 'was extremely fond of digging holes, but that form of

183

gardening was not allowed'.[229] When he grew older, this love of landscaping combined with his passion for flowing water, in a complex artificial stream. Again, it was for show, for love. He wrote about walking there with Joan or, even better, with Rosie,

> under the peach-blossom branches by the little glitter-ing stream which I had paved with crystal for them. I had built behind the highest cluster of laurels a res-ervoir, from which, on sunny afternoons, I could let a quite rippling film of water run for a couple of hours down behind the hayfield, where the grass in spring still grew fresh and deep ... And the little stream had its falls, and pools, and imaginary lakes. Here and there it laid for itself lines of graceful sand; there and here it lost itself under beads of chalcedony.[230]

He was very proud of it – the combination of fruitful soil, and delightful sound, and ingenuity, and sparkling stones. But the young women were less impressed with his labours: 'the two girls were surely a little cruel to call it "The Gutter"! Happiest times, for all of us, that ever were to be'.[231]

Memories of this work resurface in the very last chapter of his autobiography, when 'he seemed lost among the papers scattered on his table; he could not fix his mind upon them, and turned from one subject to another in despair'.[232] These luminous flowing images from his better days remained. He had hoped to build something beautiful, but he had been laughed at. It was the same story in Oxford, when he had tried to develop his love of digging into something useful.

Ruskin could never remain calmly at his desk. Walking was essential to him, and he enjoyed the opportunity to exert himself. At home, he would chop wood, and out in the fields he would slash at thistles and weeds with his stick. He decided to channel this energy into a philanthropic scheme to improve the lives of the people living in the village of Ferry Hinksey. 'For Heaven's sake – literally for Heaven's sake – let the place alone, and clean it,' he exhorted his students in a lecture in 1872.[233] He determined to improve the road in a village on the outskirts of Oxford, and initiate his young men in 'the pleasures of useful muscular work'.[234] Over the winter of 1873–4, he did gather a band of students who walked out from their colleges, picked up their shovels, and began to pave the road. It was an opportunity for them to have a conversation with Ruskin, and to put into practice some of his ideas.

In *The Crown of Wild Olive*, he had chided his audience about the wrong sort of work: why make iron railings to fence in a bit of ground where rubbish would accumulate? Why leave a stream to become choked with refuse? How could they bear it? 'The stagnant edge of the pool effaces itself into a slope of black slime, the accumulation of indolent years. Half-a-dozen men, with one day's work could cleanse those pools, and trim the flowers about their banks ... But that day's work is never given.'[235] Here at Ferry Hinksey, they could make good. Ruskin and his small band put their backs into some physical work. But they could equally easily walk away. It was not their livelihood. The road scheme was again a symbolic effort. The workers did not have to worry about putting bread on the table. They stretched their legs, made their point, and went back to their college for dinner.

For some it was a jaunt, and it ended there. For others it shaped their lives. Ruskin's biographer, William Collingwood, and his editor, Alexander Wedderburn, were among them. So was Oscar Wilde, learning to be an art critic. There were personal and political repercussions that echoed for many years. Perhaps the most impressive legacy was in the work of Toynbee Hall – named after the foreman of the Diggings, Arnold Toynbee. In 1884, a group of young graduates agreed to move into the heart of Whitechapel, one of the most deprived areas of London. Living and working alongside the poorest, they created outreach projects, sharing their skills through workshops and lectures. Their work continues today. Inspired by Ruskin's words and actions in Hinksey, many of the Toynbee Hall residents did bring about the lasting changes he had imagined. William Beveridge, the architect of the Welfare State, lived in Toynbee Hall and edited *Saint George*, the Ruskin Society journal. Clement Attlee was secretary of the Hall. He acknowledged the impact of *Unto this Last* on his own world view: 'it was through this gate, that I entered the Socialist fold.'[236]

Wealth and 'illth'

Ruskin refused to subscribe to the redistribution of wealth advocated by the Socialists. And he always maintained his faith in monarchy and hierarchies – the proper places of masters and men. But he did attempt to transform our concept of wealth. He asked, why does our society hold 'precious and beneficent things, such as air, light, and cleanliness, to be valueless'?[237] He recognised that our environment is supremely important. He knew that air and light cannot be taken for granted. The storm clouds were already gathering. Ruskin saw that our ways of working are to blame, and are unsustainable. 'Men can neither drink steam, nor eat stone,' he wrote. If no one speaks out, we are destined to 'live diminished lives in the midst of noise, of darkness, and of deadly exhalation'.[238]

His approach was anti-capitalist. He questioned what it means to be rich. 'Some treasures,' as he put it, 'are heavy with human tears.'[239] The money in our pocket is not intrinsically valuable. It is only worth something if we have it, and our neighbours do not.

Ruskin returned to his Evangelical roots, creating allegories that remind us of Bible stories. Suppose there was a person

> in possession of a large estate of fruitful land, with rich beds of gold in its gravel; countless herds of cattle in its

pastures ... but suppose, after all, that he could get no servants? In order that he may be able to have servants, some one in his neighbourhood must be poor, and in want of his gold – or his corn. Assume that no one is in want of either ... He must, therefore, bake his own bread, make his own clothes, plough his own ground, and shepherd his own flocks. His gold will be as useful to him as any other yellow pebbles on his estate. His stores must rot, for he cannot consume them. He can eat no more than another man could eat, and wear no more than another man could wear.[240]

The message in Ruskin's parable is clear. 'What is really desired, under the name of riches, is, essentially, power over men.'[241] In our culture, being rich means buying and selling another person's labour. It is built on inequality. But it is possible to sidestep this system, 'to seek – not greater wealth, but simpler pleasure; not higher fortune, but deeper felicity.' Ruskin associates these pleasures with fruitfulness, with diverse habitats, with birdsong: 'no air is sweet that is silent.'[242] Of course, his vision is idealistic, based on a utopian pre-industrial model. But it is also compelling.

Ruskin's readers have always found ways to push back against encroaching 'illth' – the word he coined for work that is negative, that causes 'devastation and trouble'. Often this is through small adjustments. They have set up a book group. Planted window boxes or allotments. Joined local wildlife projects. Cleaned a canal. Moved to Ruskin Land. Built a garden city. Campaigned for the National Health Service. None of these things are 'income-generating' in the usual sense. But they are life-enhancing. And as Ruskin said, 'there is no wealth but life'.[243]

Ruskin's four essays on political economy, published together as *Unto this Last*, came to an abrupt end. His editor refused to give any more space in the Cornhill magazine to his controversial ideas about wealth and illth. Even his father was aghast at the turn his criticism was taking. In the final article, Ruskin asked, 'What kind of person it is who usually sets himself to obtain wealth'? His answer pulled no punches.

> The persons who become rich are, generally speaking, industrious, resolute, proud, covetous, prompt, methodical, sensible, unimaginative, insensitive, and ignorant. The persons who remain poor are the entirely foolish, the entirely wise, the idle, the reckless, the humble, the thoughtful, the dull, the imaginative, the sensitive, the well-informed, the improvident, the irregularly and impulsively wicked, the clumsy knave, the open thief, and the entirely merciful, just, and godly person.[244]

It is up to us to decide. Where do we want to stand in this list? 'Luxury at present can only be enjoyed by the ignorant,' he wrote. Ruskin urges us to open our eyes to the iniquities of our current systems. Can we justify our reliance on intensive agriculture, plastics pollution, fossil fuels and fracking? Or can we, as Ruskin urges, 'raise the veil boldly; face the light.'[245] Choose life.

Chapter 8

Learning

The Dryad's Crown: Oak Leaves in Autumn

'All true opinions are living, and show their life by being capable of nourishment; therefore of change. But their change is that of a tree – not of a cloud.'[246]

Changing our minds, growing up and out, and yet still remaining rooted: Ruskin's organic image of the transforming power of learning comes in the last volume of *Modern Painters*. He had carried his readers along with him, through five fat books and twelve long years since he first embarked on the project. It had begun as a review of Turner's place in contemporary art, but Turner himself had died before the series was complete, and Ruskin's understanding of his own role as a critic had shifted dramatically. His opinions – about Turner and the Pre-Raphaelites, mountains and glaciers, myths and faith – had moved on.

In some ways *Modern Painters* and *The Stones of Venice* were Ruskin's apprentice pieces. They laid the groundwork for his more expressive, more radical maturity. They gave him the authority to step out of his study and onto the lecturing platform. As he continued to learn, and share his knowledge, Ruskin discovered a great public appetite for his observations and judgements. Geology, industrial relations, women's education, what to draw, how to draw it, the names of flowers, the passage of clouds: they all mattered to him, and his interdisciplinary approach kept his audiences on their toes. His writing was demanding, as he often wove together the deep history of words, with references to ancient legends, Biblical quotations, and scientific analogies. Ruskin refused to be contained within neat boundaries. That meant that his teaching appealed to many readers and listeners who were not conventional students. He reached working men and girls, and promoted the idea of lifelong learning. He explained the value of multisensory learning; he thought beyond books, encouraging hands-on engagement with nature and art, through gardening, making, listening, walking, questioning. His father said he could have been a bishop. Ruskin did create flowing passages that read like sermons. But he used his eloquence and curiosity to suggest new ways of looking at art and life, and religion too.

'My poor little watercress life'

Ruskin's own education was fragmentary. He was mostly taught at home with tutors, or with his cousin Mary. He briefly attended school with other boys, but came home early every day. Apart from his mother's Bible teaching, there was less rigour than we might expect. Ruskin often followed his own enthusiasms, with little interference. He spent hours outdoors, poking his stick in the soil and uncurling flower petals. In the evenings, he would sit at his little table in the corner, listening to his father reading aloud. During the day, there were quiet times at his desk: 'In the intervals of these unlaborious Greek lessons, I went on amusing myself – partly in writing English doggerel, partly in map drawing, or copying Cruikshank's illustrations to Grimm, which I did with great, and to most people now incredible, exactness'.[247]

Fairy tales, poetry and drawing, these were as important to him as formal lessons. He learnt more from Walter Scott and Byron than he did from his schoolmasters. Scott gave him a love of history – some of the very last lines he wrote in *Praeterita* are wanderings in Scott's landscape of the imagination. Byron was fierce and full of marvels. He showed Ruskin the possibilities of language: 'Byron wrote, as easily as a hawk flies and as clearly as a lake reflects, the exact truth in the precisely narrowest terms; nor only the exact truth, but the most central and useful one.'[248] Ruskin was always grateful, and a little surprised, that his parents shared Byron with him, given the sauciness of some of his themes. But his mother recognised that there were as many bold tales in the Bible as were found in *Childe Harold*, and trusted that he would come to no harm.

It was Byron, too, who helped to form Ruskin's delight in

the Alps, which became so essential to his thinking. Ruskin explained that the poet 'could not teach me to love mountains or sea more than I did in childhood', but he 'first animated them for me with the sense of real human nobleness and grief'. And then he went on, rather mournfully, 'I must get back to the days of mere rivulet singing, in my poor little watercress life'.[249]

Ruskin had no grand adventures, no Byronic encounters with bandits on his family journeys. He revelled in the glory of the mountains, but his own life was reticent. He carried this sense of inadequacy, this inability to live up to his surroundings, to Oxford. 'I was, in all sorts of ways at once, less than myself,' he wrote, 'and in all sorts of wrong places at once, out of my place.'[250] As a first generation undergraduate, Ruskin was woefully naïve. When he went up to start his studies, his mother went too. His father visited Oxford at weekends. Family life reoriented to prioritise their only child.

Ruskin wanted to justify his parents' faith in him by winning the prestigious Newdigate poetry prize. He succeeded 'on my third try . . . at last, to my father's tearful joy – and my own entirely ridiculous and ineffable conceit and puffing up'.[251] But he found, at every stage, that the process of studying at university was fraught and unsatisfactory. (He was eventually awarded an honorary double fourth-class degree.) Like many students who have always appeared to be particularly bright or precocious as children, he found that he was not such a star when he reached Christ Church.

Here, the world did not revolve around him. He had to get to grips again with the ancient texts, but rather than being liberated by his reading, he found 'the hard work on Greek and Algebra had greatly, not sobered, but, numbed me'. Looking back, he realised that he had 'spent the sunny hours of many a glorious morning' working on his poetry and 'in trying which of two fine words would fit best at the end of a stanza'. Ruskin remembered many of these months as 'a grey blight of all wholesome thought and faculty, in which a vulgar conceit remained almost my only motive to exertion'.[252] He misjudged the expectations of the other 'gentleman-commoners' by trying too hard with his essays. They derided him for 'the thoughtlessness and audacity of writing one that would take at least a quarter of an hour to read, and then reading it all'.[253] Ruskin often made the mistake of believing he could woo those he admired by bombarding them with dry prose. He tried it with Adèle, and later with Turner, and neither was impressed.

Ruskin was saved by faith and by drawing. One of the older students asked him to sketch a Norman doorway, which encouraged him to refocus on his hand skills, and to recognise the importance of accuracy in architectural studies. Ruskin's works caught the attention of a Fellow, Dr Buckland, who asked to see more of his drawings. He was able to show his portfolio, filled, according to one of the other young men at Dr Buckland's breakfast gathering, with 'very clear, minute and exceedingly beautiful details of some of the most celebrated cathedrals, churches, ruins, etc. There is great spirit, richness, and freedom of touch in his style of drawing'.[254] Here was something that was satisfying. Ruskin's eye for beauty and his ability to translate it, to make it available to others, was a great gift.

He also found respite in his opportunity to worship every day in the Cathedral. During the morning services at Christ Church he could look up and know that 'every stone, every pane of glass, every panel of woodwork, was true, and of its time ... most lovely English work both of heart and hand ... The roof was true Tudor, – grotesque, inventively constructive, delicately carved'.[255] There was so much to see. These years in Cardinal Wolsey's college were a chance to reimagine his relationship with God and the 'beauty of holiness'. Having been brought up surrounded by the sharp Protestantism of his mother, he gradually discovered other approaches to worship – in Oxford, in Abbeville and finally in Turin.

'All great Art is Praise'

Learning to doubt and to question his mother's teaching; learning to find God in unexpected places, in sensuality and colour, these were hard lessons for Ruskin. In his letters and lectures, we watch him tentatively explore the edges of a more expansive faith, until he finally plunges, heart and soul, into the delightful paintings of Veronese. As a boy, he listened and followed orders but he could not say that he loved God: 'not that I had any quarrel with Him, or fear of Him; but simply found what people told me was His service, disagreeable; and what people told me was His book, not entertaining.'[256]

Sundays, the time supposedly devoted to worship, were a trial for Ruskin, as for many children of his generation. Dreary hours spent on hard pews in church, only relieved by watching the dust rise from red velvet when the preacher struck the cushion on his lectern to make his point. Or reading at home after dinner – but only the approved texts, filled with threats and an overbearing awareness of sin:

> Mary and I got through the evening how we could, over the *Pilgrim's Progress*, Bunyan's *Holy War*, Quarles's *Emblems*, Foxe's *Book of Martyrs*, Mrs. Sherwood's *Lady of the Manor*, – a very awful book to me, because of the stories in it of wicked girls who had gone to balls, dying immediately after of fever . . . We none of us cared for singing hymns or psalms as such.[257]

The atmosphere was not even relieved by song. His experience of the divine was one-dimensional, word-based. Where was the joy, the hope of salvation? 'On the whole,' he wrote later, 'it seemed to me, all that was required of me was to say my prayers, go to church, learn my lessons, obey my parents, and enjoy my dinner.'[258]

We have already seen how Abbeville opened Ruskin's

eyes, a little, to the possibility that it could be a pleasure to spend time in church. He wrote ecstatically about the interconnection between the cathedral and the town that lay in its shadow. His enthusiasm for the Gothic architecture of France and Italy had to go hand in hand with an awareness that the pre-Reformation Catholic church could foster a living faith. After a childhood in which Roman Catholicism was feared as monstrous, Ruskin's inclination towards the medieval alarmed his mother. His wife, Effie, wrote to her parents about it: 'Mrs R. goes to such extremes of anti-Popery that I am really afraid of her tormenting John into being more with them then he otherwise would, for his vanity is terribly hurt at her speaking to him exactly like a child.'[259] It seemed to be an act of rebellion, that he should engage in debates about theology and liturgy with Catholic divines. His decision to meet Archdeacon (later Cardinal) Manning was extremely disturbing to his family – but as he pointed out, it is 'to the discredit of Protestantism that my mother is afraid after having bred me up in its purest principles for thirty-four years, to let me talk for half an hour with a clever Catholic'.[260] Ruskin needed to rethink his religious beliefs if he was ever going to transcend the limitations of his mother's horizons.

Learning to approach God in new ways, and old ways, was difficult, but Ruskin discovered that he was drawn increasingly to more ancient forms of worship. He joked with Burne-Jones that they could design a basilica, with 'a barrel roof that should hold our hierarchies and symbols and gods . . . a clear space for our histories – and beasts and things below them and a floor – O what a floor'.[261] This would be an ideal place to pray, surrounded by strange and inspiring images, and steeped in history.

Burne-Jones and his wife Georgie travelled with Ruskin, and stood by him through his intellectual and spiritual upheavals. At a particularly low point, he explained to the painter Rossetti, 'I can no more go on living as I have done. Jones will tell you what an aspen-leaf and flying speck of dust in the wind my purposelessness makes me.'[262] Throughout his later madness, Georgie reappeared in his hallucinations, as 'a continually protecting and – sometimes disagreeably Advising Matron'.[263] Afterwards, he recalled 'the great contest between the Devil and – Georgie! (who represented throughout the adverse queenly or even archangelic power) for the Kingdom of the World she raced him, and won'.[264]

The Burne-Joneses represented, to a certain extent, the family he never had, and he relied on them for emotional support. When Ruskin was making plans to retreat permanently to Switzerland, they were among the friends who persuaded him to come home. His idea of retiring from the world, like a hermit, crystallised in the weeks after Rose La Touche became seriously ill. (More than a year later, in January 1865, her mother explained that she still 'can't write or think – consecutively – so that it's just as if she's dead'.[265]) Ruskin's resistance to the strict Bible-based Protestantism

that Rose demanded caused a fundamental rift in their relationship, one that he could find no way to repair – his own
faith was so fractured. He too was exhausted and depressed,
writing to his father, 'the vital energy fails ... and then for
the rest of the day one is apt to think of dying, and of the
"days that are no more". It is vain to fight against this – a
man may as well fight with a prison wall.'[266]

The idea of escaping to his mountaintop, at this point, was
foolhardy. But it was the latest of his schemes for removing
himself from the world. At times, this desire to flee evolved
into the dream of becoming a monk. He imagined the church
as a place of sanctuary, a retreat from his personal difficulties.
Even when he was married to Effie, perhaps especially when
that marriage was failing, he voiced this hope, that he could
leave her and all his disappointments behind. 'Perhaps for
my health,' he had told his father, 'it might be better that I
should declare at once that I wanted to be a Protestant monk,
separate from my wife, and go and live in that hermitage
above Sion, which I have always rather envied.'[267]

But gradually he found ways to encompass his mutable
spirituality and his recognition of the central place of the
Creator God in his world view. Again, it was through art, his
own refocusing on the divine in the beautiful, that he found a
way to reconnect. An encounter with Veronese's *Solomon and
the Queen of Sheba* in Turin completed his 'unconversion'. He
had come away, disappointed, from a service in the local Protestant church. The sallow complacency of the preacher had

been almost unbearable. Now he found himself face to face with an ancient queen and her retinue. The window of the gallery was open, and a bold brass band provided the background music to this moment. Ruskin wrote about it many times in his afterlife. It was his personal epiphany. At last he was able to turn away from his mother and towards something grander, more alive. 'Has God made faces beautiful, and limbs strong, and created these strange, fiery, fantastic energies, and . . . created gold, and pearls, and crystal, and the sun that makes them gorgeous . . . only that all these things may lead His creatures away from Him?' He went on,

And is this mighty Paul Veronese, in whose soul there is a strength as of the snowy mountains, and within whose brain all the pomp and majesty of humanity floats in a marshalled glory, capacious and serene like clouds at sunset – this man whose finger is as fire, and whose eye is like the morning – is he a servant of the devil; and is the poor little wretch in a tidy black tie, to whom I have been listening this Sunday morning expounding Nothing with a twang – is he a servant of God?[268]

No, he could finally answer. Flesh and blood were as gorgeous and good as leaves and flowers. Fra Angelico's angels, for all their dancing delicacy, seemed 'poor weak creatures' by comparison. Ruskin embraced the fulness of God's creation. This was a turning point in his education. It took him forty years to reach this place of delight, and sadly, it slipped away from him. But while it lasted, the impact of his new clear-sightedness was extraordinary. It was the springboard for many of his revelatory writings and lectures, when he could reposition himself as a voice, not just for art and artists, but for radical change in the way the world worked.

Ruskin's belief that there was more to life than the mundane and the visible underpinned his work. He revered Turner, despite the artist's atheism, because he seemed to reveal God's hand in Creation. Looking to the heavens, Ruskin tried to show that God 'paints, – beautiful things, if you will look, – terrible things, if you will think. Fire and hail, snow and vapour, stormy wind (cyclone and other), fulfilling His Word. The Word of God, printed in very legible type of gold on lapis-lazuli, needing no translation'.[269] When he first encountered the Alps, he felt they were 'the seen walls of lost Eden'.[270] He could not escape the conviction that God and nature were intimately entwined. This pervaded all his work. Whether he was joyful or melancholy, Ruskin kept coming back to the divine.

'Sticks and stones and steep dusty road'

It was not easy. At times he was weary. He had to learn to translate this ingrained belief into positive teaching, for himself and for his readers. Ruskin still had to ask, what is the point of God if the things and people that mattered to him were passing away? How should we enjoy the blessings of this life? 'Was this grass of the earth made green for your shroud only, not for your bed? And can you never lie down *upon* it, but only *under* it?'[271] This was the question he put to his audience. It was just as important to take pleasure in gazing at the world, resting in the landscape, as it was to probe or turn a profit.

Sometimes, the problem was that the world seemed just too big to take in at a glance. However hard he looked, there was no peace for his eye. Even in the most spectacular surroundings, he could not always engage with his environment as he hoped. But he found ways to focus. He described poignantly how he learnt to concentrate on one element, to bring out the joy. He discovered the techniques of mindfulness more than a century before the term was coined. In his early thirties, Ruskin spent a summer walking high into the Alps. It seemed he 'had the whole valley of the Arve . . . Mont Blanc and all its aiguilles . . . in front of me; marvellous blocks of granite and pines beside me, and yet with all this I enjoyed it no more than a walk on Denmark Hill'. But then 'I discovered that when I confined myself to one thing – as to the grass or stones . . . or the Mont Blanc – I began to enjoy directly; because then I had mind enough to put into the thing'. He found that his spirit could 'rest contented with little, knowing that if it throw its full energy into that little, it will be more than enough'.[272] When he was disenchanted, when it seemed that 'the sunset of to-day sunk upon [him] like the departure of youth', he discovered that if he 'put [his] *mind* into the scene ... it gilded all the dead walls, and [he] felt a charm in every vine tendril that hung over them ... The whole scene without it was but sticks and stones and steep dusty road'.[273]

Ruskin's ability to fix his attention on one detail, and make it sing, was bound up with his skill as an art critic. When he was teaching his readers to draw, he advised them to look closely at one corner of a picture, and try to get to grips with that. Later, when he had lost Rose, certain symbols on the edges of paintings became disproportionately important. Ruskin began to associate Carpaccio's painting of *The Dream of St Ursula* with his affections for Rose. He made copies of the work and meditated on tiny sections: her sleeping face, the plants on the parapet, the little dog at the foot of her bed.

Ruskin's fixation on these little touches was heightened by his insanity. His readers became perplexed when he wrote about them in *Fors Clavigera*, telling his 'pretty stories' about St Ursula and 'a Venetian dog ... unconscious of the angel with the palm, but is taking care of his mistress's earthly crown'.[274] They made no sense, except to a very few friends. But his love for this young woman had permeated his thinking and writing, unseen by his audiences, from the mid-1860s. Many of his works, including 'Of Queens' Gardens' and *Proserpina* were written with Rose in mind. She renewed his interest in girls' education and helped him to understand the potential in young women. As a bright teenager, her letters inspired and rebuked him. Even after her death, he continued to frame his writings as gifts for Rose.

Queenliness

Ruskin's attitude towards women has often been criticised. His unconsummated marriage to Effie and his peculiar attachment to Rose have counted against him. His decision to treat the girls' school, Winnington Hall, as his second home when he was in his mid-forties also seems questionable. The young women who danced with him there, and listened to his tales, and inspired *The Ethics of the Dust (Ten Lectures to Little Housewives)*, his treatise on mineralogy, were strange companions for a middle-aged man. Today it is inconceivable that a headmistress would allow such unchaperoned access to her pupils. Inevitably we wonder about his motives. So is it possible, or right, to look beyond the oddity of his situation and consider his genuine concern for women's learning?

There has long been a debate about how Ruskin treated women in his writing. 'Of Queens' Gardens' seems at times to sideline girls, establishing the concept of separate spheres of action for men and women. Ruskin has been accused of seeing women only as 'helpmates', and of insisting on chivalric relations between the sexes: 'the man's power is active, progressive, defensive. He is eminently the doer, the creator, the discoverer, the defender . . . her intellect is not for invention or creation, but for sweet ordering, arrangement, and decision . . . She must be enduringly, incorruptibly good; instinctively, infallibly wise'.[275] This sounds uncomfortable to modern ears. Limiting a woman's power to the home, and expecting her to be impossibly good and wise – it is not surprising that most twenty-first-century readers give up at this point. But it is worth pressing on. Because having lulled his Victorian audience into a sense of security, Ruskin then began to describe the building blocks that supported such a virtuous woman. Education, in his view, was essential. Training the body and the brain together, insisting on 'splendour of activity and . . . physical freedom' was his first point.[276] He tried to explain that you cannot 'make a girl lovely, if you do not make her happy'. Yes, he wanted the girls he taught to look on him with 'the perfect loveliness of a woman's countenance', but he believed that this could only be achieved 'in that majestic peace, which is founded in the memory of happy and useful years'.

Ruskin went on to outline the areas of knowledge that he thought were essential for young women: foreign languages, science, geography, history and faithfulness in prayer (but not theology). 'A woman, in any rank of life,' he suggested, 'ought to know whatever her husband is likely to know, but to know it in a different way.' He went on, 'indeed, if there were to be any difference between a girl's education and a boy's, I should say that of the two, the girl should be earlier led, as her intellect ripens faster, into deep and serious subjects: and that her range of literature should be, not more, but less frivolous'. He acknowledged that girls and boys matured at different paces, and that girls would lose out if their families persisted in treating them like infants, when they were more capable than boys of their own age. There was nothing wrong in reading good modern novels. Or, even better, 'turn her loose into the old library every wet day, and let her alone. She will find what is good for her; you cannot.' Give her the chance to study art and music.

Finally he reveals his hand: 'let a girl's education be as serious as a boy's. You bring up your girls as if they were meant for sideboard ornaments, and then complain of their frivolity. Give them the same advantages that you give their brothers.' And 'give them, lastly, not only noble teachings, but noble teachers'. Ruskin turned on his listeners, who treated their governess 'with less respect than they do your housekeeper (as if the soul of your child were a less charge than jams and groceries'. He asked, 'is a girl likely to think her own conduct, or her own intellect, of much importance' if her teacher was overlooked or belittled by the rest of the family?[277]

What seemed to begin as a conventional treatise on the need for men to go out and do the dirty work, while women were protected inside the home, was soon turned on its head. Ruskin couched his proposals in neat phrases about 'delicacy' and girls growing like flowers. But in fact, he was putting forward a radical syllabus for training young women, so that they

209

could keep up with their brothers or husbands. No wonder this lecture was taken up and circulated by campaigners for women's rights. It was, on one hand, a very personal response to the damaging narrowness of Rose's own upbringing (and its devastating impact on Ruskin's happiness). Ruskin admitted that he wrote it 'to please one girl'.[278] On the other hand, 'Of Queens' Gardens' recognised the tremendous potential for good, if only more women had access to education. They would transcend their domestic sphere, using their 'power to heal, to redeem, to guide and to guard ... and be no more housewives, but queens'.[279]

Ruskin could never shake off his allegorical flourishes, which seemed sometimes to contradict the main thrust of his argument. He still imagined the relationship between women and men as complementary, rather than equal. He could not resist courtly imagery. And yet, his words were life-changing for many young women, as he outlined what a girl could do. Teenagers like Dora Livesey, Sibyl Noyes, Isabel Marshall and Lily Armstrong who helped compile his index for *Modern Painters*, or read his *Elements of Perspective*, carried his teachings with them forever. Under Ruskin's system, they were able to think and speak; they could be physically active; have access to complete libraries of books, old and new; learn to converse freely in other languages; understand the principles of the natural sciences; and recognise the importance of history in shaping our world.

'How things bind and
blend themselves together!'

When Ruskin emphasises the importance of order as one attribute of queenliness, this is not something small and limiting. For him, order is everything. The proper arrangement of relationships, between individuals, between ourselves and our environment, lies at the heart of his teaching. He writes about responsibility and the need for women, as well as men, to 'be trained in habits of accurate thought'.[280] Truth, order and accuracy: in an interconnected society, Ruskin sees that it is essential for everyone to recognise that they are accountable for their actions. We are not free agents, but part of an extended network of consumers and producers, teachers and pupils, givers and takers. Cooperation, not competition, is the key to sustainable government, working for the commonwealth. With training and good stewardship, we can make our little go further.

Ruskin had already noticed that the resources we have taken for granted are being eroded: clean air, fresh water, green grass. He tried to raise awareness, to show that 'no human being, however great, or powerful, was ever so free as a fish. There is always something that he must, or must not do ... the Sun has no liberty – a dead leaf has much'.[281] Ruskin offers us that choice – between useful, controlled, energetic life, and free-floating death. We can drift, or we can focus. Which of his 'Two Paths' will we take?

'How things bind and blend themselves together!' he wrote, at the very end of his active life. This is his lesson for us, now more urgently than ever. Ruskin was never able to extricate himself from the day-to-day, however sad he became, however much he wanted to climb to the top of a mountain, beyond the reach of his friends and critics. It was not possible. The links of mind and spirit, of place and word, were too strong and too pressing. He was heartbroken, but he persisted in trying to open his own eyes wider, to see further. And to share what he saw, to show its significance.

All too often, artists and historians step away from the big questions when they are looking at something beautiful or old or complex. They forget to ask: 'So what?' 'Why does it matter?' Ruskin never hesitated. He wanted to know, not just about the surface of something delightful to the eye, but what gave it shape; where it had come from; how it had been changed by time and weather; how it fitted into the bigger picture of the society that made it, or the mountain that it grew on, or the climate patterns that swirled around overhead. He asked: is it just? Is it true? He wanted his readers to have the tools to spot the fakes, and to speak truth to power. Ruskin refused to be complacent.

Through all of his working life, he continued to create his own form of beauty, with words and images. His own water-colours and his revelatory prose-poems are astonishingly vivid. Even at the very end, when the darkness was about to engulf him, Ruskin conjured up a ravishing description of an evening in Italy. So much had faded from his view. But this memory remained, of a stormy twilight mixed with sweet echoes of Dante. And here we will leave him, walking with an old friend, in the hills above Siena,

> where the fireflies among the scented thickets shone fitfully in the still undarkened air. *How* they shone! moving like fine-broken starlight through the purple leaves. How they shone! through the sunset that faded into thunderous night ... the fireflies everywhere in the sky and cloud rising and falling, mixed with the lightning, and more intense than the stars.[282]

Acknowledgements

Over thirty years ago, Ruskin began guiding me through art and the landscape. He was my wayfinder on my first visit to Venice, and my last tour of Florence. His thoughts on the Pre-Raphaelites and Victorian society helped to shape my own studies. I am very grateful to all the scholars and enthusiasts who have shared their knowledge and love of Ruskin with me.

Colin Harrison, Catherine Whistler and Jon Whiteley have all opened my eyes to the glories of the Ashmolean collections.

The Ruskin To-Day meetings have shown me the multi-faceted possibilities of Ruskin, and I have particularly benefited from conversations with David Barrie, Dinah Birch, Stuart Eagles, Robert Hewison, Howard Hull, Sandra Kemp, Kate Mason, Ruth Nutter, Louise Pullen and Clive Wilmer.

In York, I have been encouraged by Liz Prettejohn, and

supported in my research by Beatrice Bertram and our colleagues at York Art Gallery.

My friends, Angela, Ingrid, Amelia, Melissa and Elizabeth have never flagged in their kindness and patience. Julia has inspired me to keep writing.

I am very grateful to Ben Brock at Quercus and Jonathan Conway for suggesting that I might bring Ruskin to a wider audience, and for seeing it through. Ana McLaughlin has been unfailingly positive and open-minded about the project.

My family have borne the brunt of the years of Ruskin. My parents, Diane and Graham, have looked after us all, and made it possible for me to think in a straight line. John has been unwavering in his belief in me. And my girls, with their singing, dancing, drawing and writing have kept me smiling. They remind me every day to look to the future. Thank you.

Notes

Preface: Venetian Glass

1   *The Stones of Venice* (*Works*, vol. 10, p. 197)
2   *Modern Painters III* (*Works*, vol. 5, p. 333)
3   *The Poetry of Architecture* (*Works*, vol. 1, p. 148)
4   *Unto this Last* (*Works*, vol. 17, p. 105)
5   Peter Wardle and Cedric Quayle, *Ruskin and Bewdley* (The Guild of St George: York, 1989), reprinted 2007, p. 41

Introduction: How did Ruskin learn to look?

6   Thanks to the dedicated work of the Ruskin Library, University of Lancaster, all thirty-nine volumes have been digitised and can be downloaded as searchable PDFs. Other ways of accessing the 'Library Edition' are being investigated. Cook and Wedderburn did not include all his letters and diaries, especially those which were thought to be too sensitive, including *The Brantwood Diary*, edited by Helen Viljoen (1971) and *John Ruskin's Correspondence with Joan Severn: Sense and Nonsense Letters*, edited by Rachel Dickinson (2008)
7   *Praeterita* (*Works*, vol. 35, p. 177)
8   Ibid., pp. 107–8

9   Ibid., p. 79

10   Ibid., pp. 115–6

11   Ibid., p. 25

12   *The Laws of Fésole* (*Works*, vol. 15, p. 351)

13   *Modern Painters I* (*Works*, vol. 3, p. 104)

14   Charlotte Brontë, letter to W.S. Williams, 31 July 1848, ed. Margaret Smith, *The Letters of Charlotte Brontë: volume 2, 1848-1851* (Clarendon Press: Oxford, 2000), p. 94

15   John Ruskin, 'Statement to his Proctor', quoted in J. Howard Whitehouse, *Vindication of Ruskin* (George Allen and Unwin: London, 1950), p. 15

16   Effie Gray, quoted in Suzanne Fagence Cooper, *The Model Wife: the Passionate Lives of Effie Gray, Ruskin and Millais* (Duckworth Overlook: London, 2010), p. 80

17   *Vindication of Ruskin*, p. 15

18   *Praeterita* (*Works*, vol. 35, p. 37)

19   *The Art of England* (*Works*, vol. 33, p. 293)

Chapter 1: Seeing

20   *The Crown of Wild Olive*, Introduction (*Works*, vol. 18, p. 399)

21   Ibid., p. 392

22   *The Crown of Wild Olive*, 'Traffic' (*Works*, vol. 18, pp. 434–6)

23   *Praeterita* (*Works*, vol. 35, p. 166)

24   *The Stones of Venice* (*Works*, vol. 9, p. 72)

25   *Praeterita* (*Works*, vol. 35, p. 20)

26   Ibid., p. 132

27   Ibid., p. 36)

28   Ruskin, letter to Elizabeth Gilbert, campaigning for the Royal Association for Promoting the Welfare of the Blind, 2 September 1871

29 Stuart Eagles, private communication, 20 July 2018

30 *Fors Clavigera*, Letter 10, October 1871 (*Works*, vol. 27, p. 169)

31 *Praeterita* (*Works*, vol. 35, p. 78)

32 *Turner: The Harbours of England* (*Works*, vol. 13, p. 298)

33 Ibid., p. 111)

34 Ibid., pp. 114–17)

35 *Praeterita* (*Works*, vol. 35, p. 51)

36 Ibid., p. 161

37 The Stories of Venice (*Works*, vol. 11, pp. 186–7)

Chapter 2: Drawing

38 *Praeterita* (*Works*, vol. 35, p. 59)

39 Ibid., pp. 74–55)

40 Ibid., p. 525)

41 *Elements of Drawing* (*Works*, vol. 15, pp. 9–10)

42 Ibid., p. 85

43 John Ruskin to Dante Gabriel Rossetti, n.d. May 1855, *Letters* (*Works*, vol. 36, p. 201): 'if you think there is anything in which I can be of any use to Miss Siddal ... if you think she would like an Albert Dürer or a photograph for her own room, merely tell me, and I will get them for her.'

44 Ruskin donated important works from his own collection to the Ashmolean Museum, Oxford and the Fitzwilliam Museum, Cambridge. He also established a museum especially for the working people of Sheffield which included examples of his favourite prints

45 *Elements of Drawing* (*Works*, vol. 15, pp. 25–7)

46 Ibid., p. 13

47 Ibid., p. 25

48 Ibid., p. 35

49 Ibid., p. 35

50 *Praeterita* (*Works*, vol. 35, p. 152)

51 *Elements of Drawing* (*Works*, vol. 15, p. 39)

52 Ibid., p. 40

53 Ibid., p. 54

54 Ibid., pp. 49–50

55 *Praeterita* (*Works*, vol. 35, p. 314)

56 Ibid., p. 315

57 J.S. Mill, *Principles of Political Economy* (1848), quoted by Emma Mason in *Christina Rossetti: Poetry, Ecology, Faith* (Oxford University Press: Oxford, 2018), p. 10

58 *Elements of Drawing* (*Works*, vol. 15, p. 25)

59 *The Two Paths* (*Works*, vol. 16, p. 371)

60 *The Storm-Cloud of the Nineteenth Century* (*Works*, vol. 34, p. 28)

61 Ibid., pp. 28–9)

62 Ibid., n.p. 32–3

63 Ibid., pp. 21, 33

64 Ibid., pp. 7, 10, 40

65 Ibid., n.p. 23–4

66 Ibid., p. 26

67 *The Brantwood Diary of John Ruskin, together with selected related letters and sketches of persons mentioned*, edited and annotated by Helen Gill Viljoen (Yale University Press: New Haven and London, 1971), p. 81

68 Ibid., p. 307

69 *Deucalion* (*Works*, vol. 26, p. 253)

70 *The Brantwood Diary*, p. 545

Chapter 3: Building

71   John Ruskin to John James Ruskin, 9 August 1848, *The Seven Lamps of Architecture* (*Works*, vol. 8, p. xxix)

72   Effie Ruskin, quoted in Suzanne Fagence Cooper, *The Model Wife: the Passionate Lives of Effie Gray, Ruskin and Millais* (Duckworth Overlook: London, 2010), p. 51

73   *Praeterita* (*Works*, vol. 35, p. 157n)

74   Ibid., pp. 156–7

75   *The Seven Lamps of Architecture*, 'The Lamp of Truth' (*Works*, vol. 8, pp. 89–93)

76   Ibid., pp. 92

77   Ibid., p. 89

78   Ibid., p.92

79   *The Two Paths*, 'The Work of Iron' (*Works*, vol. 16, pp. 386–7)

80   Dante Alighieri, *Paradiso*, Canto XXXIII

81   *The Seven Lamps of Architecture* (*Works*, vol. 8, p. xxxiv)

82   *The Seven Lamps of Architecture*, 'The Lamp of Memory' (*Works*, vol. 8, p. 244–5

83   A Letter to Count Zorzi, n.d., 1877 (*Works*, vol. 24, p. 408)

84   'Circular respecting Memorial Studies of St. Mark's, Venice, now in Progress under Mr. Ruskin's Direction' (*Works*, vol. 24, p. 412)

85   Ibid., p. 412–3

86   Ibid., p. 419

87   *Praeterita* (*Works*, vol. 35, p. xxxii)

88   Effie Ruskin, letter to George Gray, 15 November 1849, quoted by Mary Lutyens, *Effie in Venice: Unpublished Letters of Mrs John Ruskin Written from Venice Between 1849 and 1852* (Pallas Editions: London, 1965), reprinted 1999, p. 69

89   *The Seven Lamps of Architecture* (*Works*, vol. 8, p. xxxii)

90 Ruskin, letter to his father, 23 Dec 1849 (*Works*, vol. 9, p. xxx)
91 *The Stones of Venice*, Arch Masonry, plate IV, (*Works*, vol. 9, after p. 168)
92 *The Stones of Venice*, The Orders of Venetian Arches, plate XIV, (*Works*, vol. 10, after p. 290)
93 *Praeterita* (*Works*, vol. 35, p. 294–5)
94 William Morris, Preface to *The Nature of Gothic* by John Ruskin (Kelmscott Press: Hammersmith 1892), p. i
95 *The Stones of Venice*, The Nature of Gothic, (*Works*, vol. 10, p. 182)
96 Ibid., pp. 206, 212
97 Ibid., p. 204
98 Ibid., p. 268
99 Ibid., p. 259
100 Ibid., p. 236
101 'The Flamboyant Architecture of the Valley of the Somme' (*Works*, vol. 19, p. 262)
102 *The Stones of Venice*, (*Works*, vol. 10, p. 437)
103 *The Stones of Venice*, (*Works*, vol. 11, p. 6)
104 Ibid., pp. 10–11
105 *The Stones of Venice* (*Works*, vol. 9, p. 17)

Chapter 4: Travelling

106 *The Stones of Venice* (*Works*, vol. 11., p. 82–3)
107 John Brunton, 'Venice poised to segregate tourists', *Guardian*, 1 May 2018; Nick Squires, 'Venice to segregate locals from tourists', *Daily Telegraph*, 25 April 2018
108 E.M. Forster, *A Room with a View* (Penguin: London, 1908; reprinted 1978), p. 39
109 William Morris, *The Lesser Arts*, lecture, 1877, reprinted by

Norman Kelvin in *William Morris on Art and Socialism* (Dover Publications: New York, 1999), p. 17

110 *Praeterita* (*Works*, vol. 35, pp. 359–61)

111 *Mornings in Florence* (*Works*, vol. 23, p. 370)

112 Ibid., pp. 379–80

113 Ibid., p. 443

114 E.M. Forster, *A Room with a View*, p. 81

115 *Mornings in Florence* (*Works*, vol. 23, p. 393)

116 Ibid., p. 393

117 *Praeterita* (*Works*, vol. 35, p. 80)

118 *Memorial Studies of St Mark's* (*Works*, vol. 24, p. 423)

119 Letter to F.W. Pullen, Secretary to the Ruskin Society of Manchester, 29 Nov 1879, *Memorial Studies of St Mark's* (*Works*, vol. 24, p. 423)

120 A Letter to Count Zorzi (*Works*, vol. 24, p. 407)

121 *Deucalion* (*Works*, vol. 26, p. 203–4)

122 *Fors Clavigera*, Letter 69, Sept. 1876 (*Works*, vol. 28, p. 699)

123 *St Mark's Rest* (*Works*, vol.24, p. 207)

124 *Praeterita* (*Works*, vol. 35, p. 33)

125 *Modern Painters III*, Introduction (*Works*, vol. 5, p. xviii)

126 *The Brantwood Diary*, 17 Feb 1878 diary entry, p. 96

127 *Praeterita* (*Works*, vol. 35, p. 111)

128 Ibid., p. 96

129 *The Two Paths*, 'The Work of Iron' (*Works*, vol. 16, pp. 376, 378)

130 Ibid., p. 379

131 *Praeterita* (*Works*, vol. 35, p. 48)

132 Ibid., p. 119

133 Simon Birch, 'Climate change is melting the French Alps, say mountaineers', *Guardian*, 24 August 2018

134 John Ruskin to Lady Simon, n.d., Ruskin Library, Lancaster, L22

135 'The Study of Architecture in Our Schools' (*Works*, vol. 19, p. 24)

Chapter 5: Loving

136 *Modern Painters II* (*Works*, vol. 4, p. 49)

137 *Praeterita* (*Works*, vol. 35, p. 14)

138 Ibid., pp. 43–6

139 Ibid., p. 26

140 Ibid., p. 94

141 Ibid., pp. 11–2

142 Ibid., pp. 123–6

143 Ibid., pp. 63–5

144 Ibid., p. 71

145 Ibid., p. 45

146 Ibid., p. 180

147 Ibid., p. 182

148 Ibid., p. 229

149 Ibid., p. 249

150 *The Model Wife: the Passionate Lives of Effie Gray, Ruskin and Millais*, p. 42

151 John James Ruskin to George Gray, 2 April 1852, Mary Lutyens (ed.), *Millais and the Ruskins* (John Murray: London, 1967), p. 5

152 John James Ruskin to George Gray, 30 March 1852, *Millais and the Ruskins*, p. 4

153 *Fors Clavigera*, quoted in introduction to *Praeterita* (*Works*, vol. 35, p. lxxv)

154 *Praeterita* (*Works*, vol. 35, pp. lxxii–lxxiii)

155 John Ruskin to Georgiana Burne-Jones, 20 July 1861, *Letters* (*Works*, vol. 36, p. 375)

156 John Ruskin to Lady Naesmyth, 22 August 1861, *Letters* (*Works*, vol. 36, p. 379)

157 John Ruskin to his father, 1 November 1861, *Letters* (*Works*, vol. 36, p. 386)

158 John Ruskin to Charles Eliot Norton, 10 March 1863, *Letters* (*Works*, vol. 36, p. 436)

159 John Ruskin to Dr John Brown, quoted in Introduction, *Praeterita* (*Works*, vol. 35, p. lxxiv)

160 *Praeterita* (*Works*, vol. 35, p. 535)

161 Ibid., pp. 538–42

Chapter 6: Losing

162 John Ruskin to Charles Eliot Norton, 30 October 1875, *Letters* (*Works*, vol. 37, p. 183)

163 *Proserpina* (*Works*, vol. 25, p. 206)

164 *Fors Clavigera*, Letter 74, February 1877 (*Works*, vol. 29, p. 30)

165 *Sesame and Lilies*, Introduction (*Works*, vol. 18, p. xix)

166 John Ruskin, letter to Joan Severn, 11 Nov 1888, quoted in *Praeterita* (*Works*, vol. 35, p. xxxiii)

167 *Praeterita* (*Works*, vol. 35, p. 558)

168 Ibid., p. 561

169 Ibid., p. 222

170 Ibid., p.70

171 John Ruskin, letter to Edward Burne-Jones, Introduction, *Sesame and Lilies* (*Works*, vol. 18, pp. xxvii–xxviii)

172 John Ruskin, letter to Dr Acland, Introduction, *Sesame and Lilies* (*Works*, vol. 18, p. xxviii)

173 *Fors Clavigera*, Letter 74, February 1877 (*Works*, vol. 29, note 18, p. 50)

174 John Ruskin, letter to George Richmond, 31 May 1878, *Letters* (*Works*, vol. 37, p. 246)

175 John Ruskin, letter to Thomas Carlyle, 23 June 1878, *Letters* (*Works*, vol. 37, p. 248–9)

176 *The Brantwood Diary*, letter to C.E. Norton, 3 Oct 1877, p. 31

177 *The Brantwood Diary*, p. 81

178 *The Brantwood Diary*, letters 10 Feb and 8 Feb 1878, and diary 12 Feb 1878, p. 63

179 *The Brantwood Diary*, 19 Feb 1878, p. 97

180 *The Brantwood Diary*, 20 Feb 1878, p. 98

181 *The Brantwood Diary*, 22 Feb 1878, p. 101

182 *The Brantwood Diary*, John Ruskin, letter to his doctor, p. 64

183 *The Brantwood Diary*, Dr Acland, letter to Gladstone, 10 March 1878, p. 66

184 *The Brantwood Diary*, Joan Severn, letter to Charles Eliot Norton, 27 March 1878, p. 68

185 *Fors Clavigera*, Letter 79, 2 July 1877 (*Works*, vol. 29, p. 160)

186 'Val D'Arno' lecture (*Works*, vol. 23, p. 49)

187 Opening Statement by William Parry, serjeant-at-law, quoted by Linda Merrill, *A Pot of Paint: Aesthetics on Trial in Whistler v Ruskin*, (Smithsonian Books: Washington and London, 1992), pp. 137–40

188 Edward Burne-Jones, quoted by Linda Merrill, *A Pot of Paint*, pp. 172–3

189 Marcel Duchamp, Tracey Emin and 'Ben' (Ben Vautier, Ecole de Nice)

190 John Ruskin, letter to Miss Susan Beever, November 1878, *Letters* (*Works*, vol. 37, p. 268)

191 *The Storm-Cloud of the Nineteenth Century* (*Works*, vol. 34, p. 24)

192 Ibid., pp. 40–43)

193 Ibid., p. 64

194 *Proserpina* (*Works*, vol. 25, pp. 221–2)

195 *The Queen of the Air*, Preface (*Works*, vol. 19, p. 293)
196 John Ruskin, letter to the Rev. J.P. Faunthorpe, 3 March 1882
(*Works*, vol. 37, p. 388)

Chapter 7: Working

197 *The Crown of Wild Olive*, Introduction (*Works*, vol. 18, pp. 391–2)
198 *Fors Clavigera*, Letter 10, Oct 1871, Vol. 27, p. 169
199 *The Stones of Venice*, The Nature of Gothic (*Works*, Vol. 10, p. 204)
200 Ibid., p. 243–4
201 Ibid., p. 205
202 Ibid., p. 235
203 Ibid., p. 237-8
204 Ibid., p. 196
205 Ibid., p. 196
206 *Unto this Last* (*Works*, vol. 17, p. 42)
207 Ibid., pp. 38–9
208 Ibid., p. 44
209 Ibid., p. 106
210 *Praeterita* (*Works*, vol. 35, p. 13)
211 *Unto this Last* (*Works*, vol. 17, p. 75)
212 Ibid., p. 35
213 Ibid., p. 113
214 Ibid., pp. 25, 29
215 *The Crown of Wild Olive* (*Works*, vol. 18, p. 393)
216 *Unto this Last* (*Works*, vol. 17, p. 104)
217 Ibid., p. 53
218 Ibid., 17, p. 89
219 Ibid., p. 102

220 *The Two Paths*, 'The Work of Iron' (*Works*, vol. 16, p. 403)

221 *Unto this Last* (*Works*, vol. 17, p. 35)

222 *Fors Clavigera*, Letter 22, October 1872 (*Works*, vol. 27, p. 381)

223 *The Two Paths*, 'The Work of Iron' (*Works*, vol. 16, p. 396)

224 Ibid., p. 400

225 *Praeterita* (*Works*, vol. 35, p. 43)

226 *Unto this Last* (*Works*, vol. 17, p. 27)

227 Ibid., p. 31n

228 *Praeterita* (*Works*, vol. 35, p. 428)

229 Ibid., p. 59

230 Ibid., p. 560

231 Ibid., p. 561

232 Collingwood, quoted in Introduction to *Praeterita* (*Works*, vol. 35, p. xxxiii)

233 *The Eagle's Nest* (*Works*, vol. 22, p. 205)

234 John Ruskin, letter to Dr Acland, 28 March 1871 (*Works*, vol. 20, p. xli)

235 *The Crown of Wild Olive* (*Works*, vol. 18, pp. 386–7)

236 Clement Attlee, quoted by Stuart Eagles, 'Political Legacies', in Francis O'Gorman (ed.), *The Cambridge Companion to John Ruskin* (Cambridge University Press: Cambridge, 2015), p. 255

237 *Unto this Last* (*Works*, vol. 17, p. 85)

238 Ibid., p. 110

239 Ibid., p. 52

240 Ibid., p. 45

241 Ibid., p. 46

242 Ibid., pp. 111–12

243 Ibid., p. 105

244 Ibid., p. 90

245 Ibid., p. 114

Chapter 8: Learning

246 *Modern Painters V* (*Works*, vol. 7, p. 9)

247 *Praeterita* (*Works*, vol. 35, p. 74)

248 Ibid., p. 145

249 Ibid., pp. 150–1

250 Ibid., p. 194

251 Ibid., p. 613

252 Ibid., pp. 612–14

253 Ibid., p. 196

254 Thomas Sopwith, quoted in John Ruskin, Introduction, *Praeterita* (*Works*, vol. 35, p. lxv)

255 *Praeterita* (*Works*, vol. 35, p. 191)

256 Ibid., p. 45

257 Ibid., pp. 72–3

258 Ibid., p. 90

259 Effie Ruskin to Mrs Gray, 26 July 1852, *Millais and the Ruskins*, p. 16

260 John Ruskin to Mrs Gray, 28 August 1852, *Millais and the Ruskins*, p. 20

261 Burne-Jones to John Ruskin, May/June 1862, quoted by Richard Dorment, *Burne-Jones and the Decoration of St. Paul's American Church, Rome*, Columbia University, Ph.D, 1976, p. 100

262 John Ruskin, letter to D.G. Rossetti, 12 July 1862 (*Works*, vol. 36, p. 411)

263 John Ruskin, letter to George Richmond, 31 May 1878 (*Works*, vol. 37, p. 247)

264 *The Brantwood Diary*, John Ruskin, letter, 21 Jan 1880, p. 69

265 Maria La Touche to George MacDonald, quoted by Derrick Leon, *Ruskin, the Great Victorian* (Routledge and Kegan Paul: London, 1949), p. 360

266 John Ruskin to John James Ruskin, 16 Dec 1863 (*Works*, vol. 36, p. 461)

267 John Ruskin to John James Ruskin, 11 Nov 1853, *Millais and the Ruskins*, p. 109

268 *Modern Painters V*, Introduction (*Works*, vol. 7, p. xl-xli)

269 *Fors Clavigera* , Letter 75, March 1877 (*Works*, vol. 29, p. 56)

270 *Praeterita* (*Works*, vol. 35, p. 115)

271 *The Crown of Wild Olive* (*Works*, vol. 18, p. 398)

272 *Modern Painters III*, Introduction (*Works*, vol. 5, p. xx)

273 Ibid., pp. xviii-xix

274 *Fors Clavigera*, Letter 74 (*Works*, vol. 27, p. 30)

275 *Sesame and Lilies*, 'Of Queens' Gardens'(*Works*, vol. 18, pp. 121–3)

276 Ibid., pp. 123–4

277 Ibid., pp. 125–33

278 *Sesame and Lilies*, Preface, 'Of Queens' Gardens'(*Works*, vol. 18, p. 47)

279 Ibid., p. 137

280 Ibid., p. 126

281 *The Two Paths*, 'The Work of Iron' (*Works*, vol. 16, pp. 407–8)

282 *Praeterita* (*Works*, vol. 35, p. 562)